THE BEST OF
GOAN
COOKING

THE BEST OF
GOAN
COOKING

Gilda Mendonsa

UBS Publishers' Distributors Pvt. Ltd.

5 Ansari Road, Daryaganj, New Delhi-110 002
Phones: 011-23273601-4, 23260232, 23273552

(Export Division)
First Floor, MPL No. 4948, Plot No. 47, Opposite Hindi Park,
Daryaganj, New Delhi - 110 002 (India) • Phones: 011-23266646-47

9, Ashok Nagar, Near Pratibha Press, Gautam Buddha Marg, Latouche Road,
Lucknow-226 018 • Phones: 0522-4025124, 4025134

Z-18, M.P. Nagar, Zone-I, Bhopal-462 011
Phones: 0755-4203183, 4203193, 2555228

1st Floor, Shop No. 133-134, Aust Laxmi, Apparel Park, Outside Dariyapur Gate,
Ahmedabad-380 016 • Phones: 079-22160371-73, 29092241, 29092248, 29092258

2nd Floor, Shree Renuka Plaza, Tilak Road, Mahal, Nagpur-440 002
Phones: 0712-6457909, 2736010

2nd Floor, Apeejay Chambers, 5 Wallace Street, Fort, Mumbai-400 001
Phones: 022-66376922-23, 66102067, 66102069

680 Budhwar Peth, 2nd Floor, Near Appa Balwant Chowk, Pune-411 002
Phone: 020-24461653

Crescent No. 148, 1st Floor, Mysore Road, Bangalore-560 026
Phones: 080-26756377, 26756362

60 Nelson Manickam Road, Aminjikarai, Chennai-600 029
Phones: 044-23746222, 23746351-52

2nd & 3rd Floor, Sri Guru Towers, No.1-7 Sathy Road, Cross III, Gandhipuram,
Coimbatore-641 012 • Phones: 0422-2499916-17

No. 40/8199A, 1st Floor, Public Library Building, Convent Road, Ernakulam-682 035
Phones: 0484-2353901, 2363905

3rd & 4th Floors, Alekhya Jagadish Chambers, H.No.4-1-1058, Boggulkunta, Tilak
Road, Hyderabad-500 001 • Phones: 040-24754473-74

1st Floor, Plot No. 145, Cuttack Road, Bhubaneshwar-751 006
Phones: 0674-2314446-47

8/1-B Chowringhee Lane, Kolkata-700 016
Phones: 033-22529473, 22521821, 22522910

1st Floor, House No. 4, Kanaklata Path, Lachit Nagar, Bharalupar, Guwahati-781 007
Phones: 0361-2461982-83

Ground Floor, Annapurna Complex, Naya Tola, Patna-800 004
Phones: 0612-2672856, 2673973, 2686170

Visit us at www.ubspd.com & www.gobookshopping.com

© Gilda Mendonsa

First Published	1995	Tenth Reprint	2003
First Reprint	1995	Eleventh Reprint	2004
Second Reprint	1995	Twelfth Reprint	2005
Third Reprint	1995	Thirteenth Reprint	2006
Fourth Reprint	1997	Fourteenth Reprint	2007
Fifth Reprint	1998	Fifteenth Reprint	2007
Sixth Reprint	1998	Sixteenth Reprint	2009
Seventh Reprint	1999	Seventeenth Reprint	2010
Eighth Reprint	2000	Eighteenth Reprintt	2010
Ninth Reprint	2001	Ninteenth Reprint	2012

ISBN 978-81-7476-028-9

Photographs: Wilfred Goes

Printed at: Millenium Offset Pvt. Ltd., A-49, Naraina Industrial Area, Phase-I, New Delhi

Contents

Foreword

They say that "the taste of the pudding is in the eating". As someone who has dined and wined at the Mendonsa's on almost all my trips to Goa in recent years, I can vouch for the fact that I have literally devoured this fabulous cook book page by page at Gilda's dining table. I have also had sozzled experiences with Liber's *feni*-cocktails that have smuggled themselves into the book.

Gilda's book is appropriately called *The Best of Goan Cooking*. Browsing through the recipes, I walked down memory lane to a time 50 years ago. It is the month of May. The family had changed trains at Poona and Londa, gone through Portuguese Customs at Castlerock, made a sweaty, smelly bus trip to Old Goa, taken a *voddem* or canoe to cross the Mandovi to the island of Divar, and after walking the mud road across the rice fields, arrived at the ancestral home in a state of welcome, joyous unconsciousness.

My grandmother cries a little, hugs a little, and with her army of *mundkars* outside the house and a squadron of domestic help inside the house commences the Goan revival (taken from the pages of Gilda's book) of her prodigal grand children.

It starts with a jugful of *sangria,* an inspiring drink for perspiring people (see Gilda's recipe). After mangoes, hand-plucked from ancestral trees, you walk down to the well for the unforgettable experience of a family that stays together as it bathes together. The clak-clak of the pulley, the *tambeo* or copper pot hitting the clear surface of water from an eternal spring, the hiss of coir rope and screams and laughter as the cold fresh water pours over your tired head.

From then on a month long feast for the Gods... *pez* or *kanji* with yesterday's prawn curry (*kalchi kodi*) or fried prawns or *parra*. After a game of truc or flush where you cheat like hell, move on to *caldo verde* served to you at the card table. Later you sit at the dining table and choose from appetizing Portuguese-Goan dishes like *caldeirada* and *Arroz* to truly spicy Goan delicacies, 'cabidel' with whole wheat bread (*poie*). For me, a mind- blowing experience.

If you love good food, you are in some way a little Emperor whether you are a bank clerk, cancer specialist, professor, musician, or hockey player. Because Goan cuisine pampers your palate, bows to your whimsical needs and massages you into a state of drowsiness only to wake you up to a feast of tea-time sweets, *doce de grao* and *bibinca* being my down to earth favourites.

For dinner, start with *uräc* or *feni*. Nothing can beat a good *uräk*. Our ancestors looked down on the *caju* distillations which they used mostly for medicinal purposes or served to the *mundkars*. They drank *Maciera* a lousy brandy which they drank with soda and very wisely they drank *tinto*, *branco*, moscatel with their meals. Wine is the right drink at a Goan meal. Large quantities, preferably. As a result old Goans never die, they just stumble and stagger away.

If after following Gilda's recipes meticulously, the dish does not come out "finger licking" you have probably forgotten the most important ingredient. Large quantities of love. Goan cooking is family cooking ... in crowded sweaty, smoky kitchens, with earthern pots and gigantic grinding stones, where mothers, daughters and grandaunts step on each others' toes, poke their noses into each pot, squabble over the ingredients and the choice of boy-friends and allow generous helpings' of their sweat, tears and caring to mix with what will become the piece-de-resistance for any Home Coming.

If Gilda forgot to mention love and caring, she took it for granted. There is so much of it in a family of which Liber is the Lord, but Gilda is the Master! Master of the art of Goan cooking.

— **George Menezes**

Introduction

Goan hospitality is legendary, enhanced as it is by the serenity of its village life and the invigorating tang of the sea water and air, that makes the traditional meal of "fish curry and rice" a daily delight.

The Goan housewife has had plenty of practice in culinary wizardry, for unexpected guests are a frequent occurrence in this land which has preserved the gentle arts of "visiting", conversation and, above all, a keen interest in food and drink.

The intermingling of Arabian, Portuguese and native cultures is reflected in the cuisine of Goa, which is a unique blend of richness and simplicity — the two constantly recurring notes being struck by fish and the coconut. Goa is also unique in the mixture of East and West co-existing in a friendly lifestyle. The best of both worlds has been absorbed and knit into a culture distinctly different from that of any other part of India. Christian and Hindu festivals are celebrated by all, and no Goan is too busy to drop his work for a party.

Music is in every Goan's blood: Goan folk dances and the traditional songs of the fisher folk and the sowers of rice are included in every festive occasion, from a family gathering to a wedding. Young and old warble the nostalgic melodies to the accompaniment of the guitar or the *gumat* (a drum fashioned from a red clay pot) until dawn, aided by copious libations of *feni* for the gentlemen and wine for the ladies.

In the villages, food is generally cooked on wood fires in clay pots that are fashioned and fired indigenously by the village potter. This art is handed down reverently from one generation to another, and homesick Goans the world over dream about the simple life and food of their childhood days, trying to re-create the smoky flavour of the mid-day curry and the glass of fresh toddy, before abandoning all caution and buying a plane ticket to the real thing.

In the context of today's increasingly complex lifestyle, the Goan village preserves the tradition of wood fires and clay pots. Whole families make regular pilgrimages to the ancestral village home, generally to celebrate the annual feast of the patron saint of the village. The jollity and vigour of a village feast celebrated in the "old way" is an unforgettable experience.

The popularity of *feni*, the native drink of Goa, is attested to by the fact that practically every third little house is a "taverna". *Feni* is considered a cure-all for any ailment, which is a good excuse for the serious connoisseur! Coconut *feni* is made from toddy, the fermented sap of the coconut tree; cashew *feni* is the fermented juice of the cashew fruit. Every cashew fruit (when ripe, a luscious orange-gold colour, the shape of a green or red pepper) has a single nut suspended from it.

I have tried to include as wide a representation of Goan dishes in this book as possible, to suit every occasion. Do follow the recipes faithfully, and, with experience, you will be able to add a potent new string to your culinary bow.

I dedicate this book to my family (which now includes grandchildren), who have been my kindest critics.

Bon appetit!

— **Gilda Mendonsa**

Appetizers

'The first draught serveth for health, the second for pleasure, the third for shame, and the fourth for madness'....Anacharsis.

Cocktails

Feni Cocktails are a MUST in every cocktail bar of every hotel in Goa. The rating doesn't matter! They are easy to prepare even at home for a special occasion, and delightful to behold if presented well. These cocktails sharpen one's appetite for food, be it lunch, snacks or dinner, and the conversation sparkles. You now imagine yourself in the Land of Milk and Honey — the Utopia we all dream of. Here's a toast to a wonderful Time. "VIVA!"

Tips

1. Always use lots of ice.
2. Chill the glass before use, if possible.
3. Make sure you have ALL the ingredients ready in advance.
4. Take time over the presentation of the drink served.
5. Using an exotic shape and size of glass is fun, and adds to the enjoyment of the drink.
6. For an authentic touch, use the hollowed out green coconut shell, with the sides sliced off for the cocktail.

Sangria

YOU NEED:

✪ 1 cup water ✪ 1 dessertspoon sugar
✪ 2" piece cinnamon ✪ 1 large, ripe orange
✪ 1 tablespoon brandy ✪ Ice cubes
✪ 1 bottle red wine

This refreshing drink comes from an old recipe from "those were the days" of the 40's and earlier. It was made to welcome homecoming relatives and guests. Children were given a sip or two as an indulgence. The magic still holds.

METHOD:

Boil water with sugar and crushed cinnamon for 5 minutes. Cool. Lightly crush the orange, with its peel, and place the orange in a jug with the above mixture. Add the brandy and about 10 ice cubes. Stir well and top with the red wine. Serve cold in small glasses, after 15 minutes.

Serves 12 *Preparation Time* **: 15 minutes**

Fidalgo's Punch

Put ice in a tall glass.
Add 1 measure of Coconut *Feni*, 1 measure of rum, juice of half a lemon, two dashes of Angostura Bitters, 1 teaspoon of sugar. Stir and top with 2 measures of orange juice, a sprinkling of nutmeg.

Decorate with a slice of orange and a sprig of mint.

The Goan Punch

Fill a glass quarter full of ice cubes. Pour over it 2 measures of Coconut *Feni*, 1 measure of Coffee liqueur.

Stir well and serve

Sun Kiss'd Cocktail

Mix:

2 measures of coconut cream with 1 measure of Coconut *Feni*, 2 measures of pineapple juice and 4 cubes of ice in a blender. Pour into a suitable glass quarter filled with ice cubes.

Decorate with a wedge of pineapple and a cherry.

Holiday Sparkle

Pour

1 measure of Coconut *Feni* into a tall glass with plenty of ice. Add 1 teaspoon of sugar and the juice of half a lemon. Stir and top with 1 measure of dry sparkling wine.

Sol de Orange

Pour
1 measure of Coconut *Feni* into a tall glass with plenty of ice.
Top with 2 measures of orange juice. Garnish with a slice of orange.

For a longer drink...
Top with lemonade or soda-water

Tambre Maria

Pour
1 measure of Coconut *Feni* over ice cubes ($^1/_3$ glass) in a glass.
Add a dash of Worcestershire Sauce and a dash of lemon juice.
Spice with a pinch of salt, pepper, ½ teaspoon sugar and a dash of Tabasco Sauce.
Top with 2 measures of chilled tomato juice. Stir well

Decorate with fresh celery and a sprig of mint.

Frozen Pineapple

Take
A slice of pine apple and cut into chunks and blend for 20 seconds,
with 3 teaspoons of sugar, 1 measure of lemon juice, and 1 measure of Coconut *Feni*.
Fill a tall glass with half a cup of cracked ice, and pour contents over the ice.

Decorate with half a ring of pineapple.

Song of Goa

Pour

2 measures of black tea, 2 measures of orange liqueur and some lemon peel into a saucepan. Heat the contents and then take off heat. Add 2 measures of Coconut Feni. Serve in glasses ¾ filled with ice cubes.

Serves two

Guaranteed to make you sing till the wee hours of the morning.

Orchata

This is a drink originally made with almonds. Since almonds are expensive, cashewnuts as well as essence can be substituted. Orchata has a cooling effect on a hot summer day. It contains no alchohol.

YOU NEED:

- 350 gms. cashewnuts (not roasted)
- 8 cups water ○ 6½ kgs. sugar
- 4 tablespoons rosewater or orange flower water
- 1 tablespoon almond essence ○ 1 tablespoon citric acid.

METHOD:

Remove skins of cashewnuts. Soak in 2 cups of water overnight. Next morning, liquidise the soaked cashewnuts in a blender/grinder, adding an additional 2 cups of water. Mix thoroughly and put through a fine sieve. Add the rest of the water to the sieved mixture along with the sugar in a deep pan on a medium flame. Stir cook till the mixture boils for 10 minutes. Add the essence and citric acid after removing it from the heat. Cool and bottle.

To serve: To one tablespoon of Orchata concentrate add a cup of cold water and a cube of ice. Stir.

Preparation Time : **20 minutes**   *Cooking Time* : **15 minutes**

N. B. If you make Orchata with almonds, then add only 1 teaspoon of Almond essence.

Starters

While imbibing *feni*, the guest is treated to an array of mouthwatering Goan snacks. These are unique to Goa and never quite taste the same anywhere else.

Rissóis de Camarão

YOU NEED:

○ ½ cup water with salt to taste ○ 1 cup cleaned, deveined prawns
○ 1 medium onion, chopped fine ○ 1tablespoon oil
○ 1 tablespoon grated cheddar cheese ○ 2 tablespoons milk
○ 1 tablespoon cornflour ○ 1 tablespoon butter

METHOD:

In the salt water, boil the prawns which have been cut fine. Stir cook till all the water has been absorbed. Keep aside. Heat the oil on medium heat and saute the onions till they are a golden brown. Add prawns, cheese, and the cornflour mixed in the milk. Add salt to taste and stir fry for a minute. Keep aside.

For the dough you need:

○ Half cup water with salt to taste
○ 1 tablespoon butter ○ 2 cups flour
○ 2 eggs beaten ○   ½ cup breadcrumbs ○ 1 cup oil

METHOD:

In a pan, boil the water, adding the butter and the flour gradually, till all the flour had been used. The mixture should be smooth. Stir cook for 2 minutes. Cool the dough. Roll out on a floured board, and cut into small circles (App. 1½" in diameter). Place half a teaspoon of the prawn filling in one half of the circle. Press over the folded edge, sealing firmly. Now dip each *rissóis* in the egg mixture, then in the bread crumbs. Use up all the dough . Heat the oil in a pan on medium heat and fry the *rissóis* to a golden brown.

Serves 6

You should get 20 *rissóis*

Preparation Time : **30 minutes**   *Cooking Time* : **20 minutes**

The *rissóis* can be prepared in advance and heated up in the oven before serving.

Salt-Fish Balls

You Need:

✪ 4 salted, dried mackerels/250 gms. any other dried, salted fish
✪ 2 cups water ✪ 5 onions, chopped very fine
✪ 6 cloves garlic, chopped fine
✪ 6 green chillies, deseeded, chopped very fine
✪ 2 eggs ✪ 1 egg, beaten
✪ 1 kg. potatoes, boiled and mashed well
✪ Salt and pepper to taste ✪ Some rice flour
✪ 2 cups oil.

Method:

Soak fish overnight in the water. The next morning, boil the fish in the same water for 15 minutes. Remove all the bones after draining the fish, and mince the fish. Now mix all the ingredients together except the beaten egg, rice flour and oil. Form into walnut-size balls, dip into the beaten egg and then dust with rice flour. Heat oil on medium flame and deep fry the balls. Serve hot or cold with Sour-Hot Sauce.

Sour-Hot Sauce

You Need:

✪ 2 dessertspoons peppercorns ✪ 20 dried red chillies
✪ 8 cloves garlic ✪ 1" fresh ginger
✪ Salt to taste ✪ 2 lemon size of balls of tamarind
✪ ½ cup water ✪ ½ cup vinegar

Method:

Put all the above ingredients into a mixer/ blender and blend till a smooth sauce is obtained. This sauce is also excellent as a marinade for sliced/whole fish before frying.

Serves : 8   *Preparation Time : 20 minutes*   *Cooking Time : 25 minutes*

Mandaré

YOU NEED:

✪ 1 kg. orange pumpkin ✪ 1 cup water
✪ 2 level teaspoons salt ✪ 2 cups rice flour
✪ Oil, for frying

METHOD:

Remove the skin of the pumpkin and cut into cubes. Add salt to the water and put in a pan on moderate flame and boil till all the water had been absorbed. Cool and sieve the pulp. Now add the rice flour and mix thoroughly into a smooth dough, adding a little water if necessary and half a teaspoon of turmeric powder. Roll out the dough thinly on a floured board and cut into 2" circles. Arrange these on greased butter paper and keep them in the sun for 3 to 4 days till thoroughly dried. Remove gently from the greased butter paper and store in air-tight tins/ jars. Deep fry in hot oil on a moderate flame when needed. About 2-3 per person is reasonable.

Preparation Time : **40 minutes**   *Cooking Time* : **10 minutes**

Croquettes

YOU NEED:

✪ 1 kg. minced mutton or beef ✪ 2 onions, cut fine
✪ 2 red chillies (dried) ✪ 4 green chillies, deseeded
✪ 10 cloves ✪ 1" piece ginger ✪ 8 cloves garlic
✪ Salt & pepper to taste ✪ 2 slices bread ✪ 2 eggs
✪ 1 cup water ✪ Half a cup of bread crumbs ✪ 1 cup of oil for frying.

METHOD:

Mix the meat, onion, chillies, cloves, garlic, ginger and salt and pepper with 1 cup of water. Put in a pan on moderate heat and stir cook till all the water has been absorbed and the meat is dry.

Grind meat fine in a blender. Soak the bread in water for 5 minutes. Squeeze dry and add to the meat along with 1 egg, lightly beaten. Form the meat into cocktail-type sausage shspes. Beat the remaining egg and dip each croquette into the beaten egg, then into the bread crumbs. Heat the oil in a frying pan on a moderate flame and fry the croquettes to a golden brown colour. Cool. You should get about 30 croquettes.

Serves : **10**   *Preparation Time* : **30 minutes**   *Cooking Time* : **20 minutes.**

Mussels In Shell

You need:

✪ 24 large mussels in shells
✪ Salt ✪ 4 red dried chillies or peppers
✪ 8 cloves garlic ✪ ½" piece ginger
✪ ¼ teaspoon garam masala
✪ ¼ teaspoon cummin seeds ✪ 2 tablespoons vinegar
✪ ½ teaspoons sugar ✪ Salt to taste
✪ ¼ cup of oil for cooking ✪ 1 onion, cut fine

METHOD:

Wash and clean the mussels thoroughly, being careful to remove the tiny bunch of hairs in each one. Apply salt to the mussels and keep aside. Keep 24 half shells. Wash these thoroughly, and dry them and keep aside to be used later. Grind all the spices in the vinegar, adding the sugar and salt to taste. Marinate the mussels in the ground spices for 2 hours. Heat oil on a moderate flame in a frying pan. Sauté the onion and add the mussels. Stir fry for 10 minutes till well cooked and soft. Now, in each half shell, place a mussel, and decorate with a sprig of parsley or coriander.

Serves : **12** *Preparation Time* : **minutes** *Cooking Time* : **15 minutes**

N.B. In Goa, the fisherwoman who sells these mussels cleans them for her customers. Otherwise, it is difficult and tedious cleaning them at home.

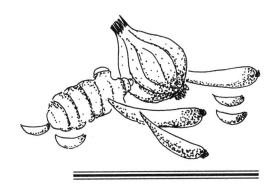

Baked Caranguejos (Crabs)

You Need:

○ 12 large crabs ○ 1 tablespoon butter
○ 2 medium onions, chopped fine
○ 2 large tomatoes, chopped fine
○ 2 green chillies or peppers, deseeded and chopped fine
○ 6 cloves garlic, chopped fine
○ ½" piece ginger, chopped fine
○ Salt and pepper to taste
○ A few parsley or coriander leaves, chopped fine
○ 2 eggs ○ 2 tablespoons of breadcrumbs

Method:

Wash the crabs thoroughly in running water. Put them in a deep pan, cover with water and add ½ teaspoon salt. Boil on high heat for 15 minutes. Cool. Remove the flesh from the shell, including that of the claws and legs. Keep only the large outer shell and dispose of the rest. In a pan, melt the butter on a medium flame. Add the onions, tomatoes, chillies or peppers, garlic and ginger. Saute till a thick paste is obtained. Stir cook continuously. Add salt and pepper, parsley or coriander, and lastly, the shredded crab meat. Stir cook for 1 minute. Remove from heat. Now mix I egg in the crab mixture. Fill each shell with the crab meat, levelling the top of each. Beat the remaining egg and brush the top of each filled shell with the egg and pat over the breadcrumbs. Heat oven to 350F, 180°C then dot the tops of the shells with butter. Arrange crab shells on a baking tray and bake for 12 minutes. Serve one crab shell per guest with sliced cucumber salad.

Serves 12   *Preparation Time* : 40 minutes   *Cooking Time* : 12 minutes

King Prawns

YOU NEED:

○ 24 king sized prawns ○ 4 red dried chillies or peppers
○ 8 cloves garlic ○ ½" piece ginger ○ ¼ teaspoon garam masala
○ ¼ teaspoon cummin seeds ○ 2 tablespoons vinegar
○ ½ teaspoon sugar ○ salt to taste ○ ½ cup oil ○ 1 onion cut fine
○ toothpicks 6" long, made from bamboo slivers.

METHOD:

Wash the prawns thoroughly. Very carefully, with a sharp knife, make a cut down the centre of the prawn on the *outer* side. Remove the dark vein. Keep aside. Grind the ginger, garlic and all the spices in the vinegar, adding the salt and sugar. Insert the toothpick through the centre of the prawn starting at the tail end and bringing it through the head. Marinate the prawns in the ground spices for 2 hours. Heat oil in a frying pan on moderate heat, and fry the king prawns, turning them carefully over till the prawns are cooked. Arrange two prawns on each plate with a fresh green salad.

Serves : 12 *Preparation Time* : 30 minutes *Cooking Time* : 20 minutes

Stuffed Papads

YOU NEED:

○ 12 small *papads* ○ ½ cup shelled prawns
○ 2 large onions, cut fine ○ 2 green chillies or peppers, cut fine
○ 4 cloves garlic ○ salt to taste ○ one cup oil.

METHOD:

Wash and devein the prawns and cut them up fine. Cut the chillies and garlic fine. Heat 1 tablespoon of oil in a pan on medium heat. Sauté the onion, garlic and chillies till golden brown. Add prawns and salt to taste. Stir fry for 7 minutes.

Moisten each *papad* carefully with a wet kitchen cloth towel. Place a teaspoonful of the prawn mixture at one end of the papad. Now roll the papad, turning in the top and bottom end, so the prawn mixture does not escape. Secure each *papad* with a toothpick. Heat oil in a frying pan on medium heat, and fry the papads carefully, turning them over till they are crisp and golden brown in colour. Fry a few at a time.

Makes 12 rolls *Preparation Time* : 30 minutes *Cooking Time* : 10 minutes

Fried Fish Platter

You Need:

✪ 8 fish fillets   ✪ 12 large prawns
✪ 12 large oysters ✪ 12 large mussels
✪ 1 tablespoon of lemon juice
✪ Salt and pepper to taste ✪ ½ cup oil
✪ 2 eggs, lightly beaten
✪ ½ cup of breadcrumbs
✪ 1 lemon & sprigs or coriander or parsley

Method:

Pat dry the fish fillets and cut into fingers. Shell and devein the prawns. Wash and pat dry. The oysters and mussels are also to be shelled, cleaned and washed. Pat dry. Marinate all the fish in the lemon juice with salt and pepper to taste. Heat oil in a pan on medium heat. Dip the fish fingers in the beaten egg, then roll in the breadcrumbs and fry to a light golden brown, turning over so both sides are done. Turn out onto a sheet of kitchen paper to absorb the extra oil. Do likewise for the oysters, mussels and prawns, in that order. Serve on a platter garnished with lemon wedges and sprigs of coriander or parsley.

Serves : 6   *Preparation Time* : **20 minutes**   *Cooking Time* : **20 minutes**

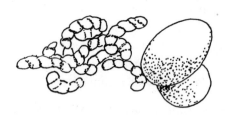

Soups

Soup, as the first course of a meal in a Goan home, originated with the serving of *pez*, a rice gruel, served in all village homes at eleven every morning, usually accompanied by a piece of mango water pickle and / or yesterday's fish curry heated and cooked till it dried up. It was a welcome interlude in the life of the busy housewife and children. To this humble bowl of *pez* was added vegetables, beans, bits of meat or fish, to make it a meal in itself. This soup came to be called *sopa grossa*. Each housewife has her own version of *sopa grossa*. She may add macaroni meat or vegetable stock to it and garnish it with croutons.

Sopa Grossa

You Need:

- 4 cups stock, (chicken, mutton, beef or vegetable)
- 2 tablespoons rice
- 50 gms each french beans, spring onions, cabbage
- ½ cup shelled green peas
- 2 tablespoons chick peas, soaked overnight & boiled
- 2 tablespoons rice
- 2 tomatoes
- Half cup boiled and diced chicken or beaf or mutton
- Salt to taste

Method:

Wash the rice and put it in with the stock in a deep pan on medium heat to cook. Chop all the vegetables fine and add to the boiling stock, with the green peas and chick peas. Stir cook till the rice is soft. Add the meat. Stir cook till the *sopa grossa* is thick and well cooked.

N.B. You may add a knob of butter if preferred, and shell fish instead of meat.

Serves : **10**   *Preparation Time* : **20 minutes**   *Cooking Time* : **30 minutes**

Caldo

You Need:

- 4 cups chicken stock
- ¾ cup milk
- salt and pepper to taste
- 1 heaped tablespoon cornflour
- ¼ cup grated cheddar cheese

No wedding buffet or important celebration is complete if this special soup, *Caldo* is not on the menu. Great attention is given to its preparation, giving it just that desired amount of piquancy. Serve with *bolinhas de queijo* or cheese balls.

Method:

In a deep pan, heat 3½ cups stock on medium heat. Add the milk, salt and pepper. When this boils, add the cornfour diluted it ½ cup of stock. Stir cook for another 5 minutes, then add the grated cheese. Remove. Serve with *bolinhas de queijo* or cheese balls.

Bolinhas de Queijo

You Need:

- ½ cup flour, sieved
- ½ tablespoon butter ● Salt to taste
- 1 cup oil

Method:

Mix together all the ingredients except the oil. Add a little water to make a smooth dough. Keep aside for 15 minutes. Now form the dough into tiny marble size balls. Keep aside for 2 hours. Now heat oil on medium heat in a deep pan and deep fry the *bolinhas de queijo*.

Serve the soup hot with a few *bolinhas de queijo* in each bowl.

Serves 10   *Preparation Time* : 30 minutes   *Cooking Time* : 25 minutes.

Canja de Galinha

You Need:

✪ Approx 300 gms chicken

✪ 1 dessertspoon oil ✪ medium onion, chopped fine ✪ 4 cloves garlic, chopped fine

✪ ¼ teaspoon turmeric ✪ ½ cup green peas ✪ Salt and pepper to taste

Method:

Boil the chicken in a pan with 4 cups of water till the meat comes easily off the bones. Cool and then cut the meat into tiny pieces. Keep aside. In another small pan, heat the oil and saute the onion and garlic cut fine, till they are a golden brown. Remove from the pan and add this to the chicken stock in the pan, along with the cleaned, washed rice, green peas, turmeric, salt and pepper. Lastly add the chicken bits and cook a further 10 minutes, till the soup thickens and the rice is soft.

Serves 6   Preparation Time : 20 minutes   Cooking Time : 20 minutes

Shellfish Soup

This soup can be prepared with 2 cupfuls of the tiny shellfish caught fresh on the Goa beaches at low tide, or with prawns or mussels.

You need:

✪ 1 cup cleaned mussels or deveined prawns

✪ ½ cup rice ✪ 2 cups water ✪ 2 tablespoons oil

✪ ½ cup finely chopped onions ✪ 6 cloves garlic, chopped fine

✪ ½" piece ginger, chopped fine ✪ a pinch of *garam masala*

✪ 2 tablespoons of dry white wine ✪ salt to taste

Method:

Wash and cook rice in 2 cups water till soft. Heat oil in a pan on medium heat and sauté onion, garlic and ginger. Add this to the rice mixture and stir cook for 5 minutes. Now add the mussels or prawns, wine, salt to taste and the *garam masalas*. Let the soup simmer on a low flame for 10 minutes. Remove.

Serves 6   Preparation Time : 20 minutes   Cooking Time : 30 minutes

Note: If the small shellfish are being used, they must be washed thoroughly, and then boiled in 2 cups of water. This will open out the shellfish, and the meat inside can be extracted. A long process but very rewarding.

Caldo Verde

YOU NEED:

- 3 large potatoes, boiled
- 1 tablespoon oil ✪ 1 large onion cut fine
- 6 cloves garlic, cut fine
- 3 cups of meat or vegetable stock
- salt and pepper to taste
- 2 cups spinach, finely cut

METHOD:

Wash and sieve the potatoes. heat the oil in a pan on medium heat and sauté onion and garlic, till golden brown in colour. To this add the stock, sieved potatoes, salt and pepper. Lastly, add the spinach. Stir cook gently till well done, for about 10 minutes. Serve hot with a knob of butter and a sprinkling of grated nutmeg.

Serves 6   *Preparation Time* : **20 minutes**   *Cooking Time* : **20 minutes**

Sopa de Cenouva

YOU NEED:

- ½ kg. carrots ✪ 4 cups meat or vegetable stock
- 1 tablespoon oil ✪ 1 large onion, chopped fine
- 4 cloves garlic, chopped fine ✪ 2 medium tomatoes, chopped fine
- 1 tablespoon flour ✪ 2 level teaspoons sugar
- ½ cup milk ✪ salt to taste
- 1 dessertspoon of butter
- ¼ teaspoon grated nutmeg

METHOD:

Wash and grate carrots. Boil grated carrots in the stock till very soft (approximately 10 mins.). Sieve the boiled mixture. Heat oil in a pan on medium heat. Sauté onion, garlic and tomatoes. Stir fry for 3 minutes till a thick pulp is obtained. Add the flour gradually, and stir fry for 1 minute. Add the carrot mixture, sugar, milk, salt and butter. Stir cook for a further 10 minutes. Add the grated nutmeg. Remove. Can be served with bread croutons if desired.

Serves 8   *Preparation Time* : **15 minutes**   *Cooking Time* : **25 minutes**

Sopa de Cebola

You need:

✪ 2 tablespoons butter ✪ 2 cups finely cut onions
✪ 4 cloves garlic, cut fine ✪ 1 tablespoon flour ✪ 1 teaspoon sugar
✪ 2 cups beef or mutton or chicken stock ✪ 1 cup water
✪ salt and pepper to taste
✪ 2 tablespoons dry, red wine ✪ 1 cup bread croutons.

METHOD:

Heat the butter in pan and sauté onions and garlic on medium heat till golden brown. Add the flour gradually till well combined. Stir fry, adding the sugar, stock and 1 cup of water, salt and pepper and the wine. Simmer on low flame for 30 minutes. Serve with croutons.

Serves : 8   Preparation Time : 20 minutes   Cooking Time : 40 minutes

Sopa de Ervilhas

You need:

✪ 1 cup dried peas ✪ 1 tablespoon oil
✪ 1 onion ✪ 3 cups water
✪ 3 soup cubes (chicken or vegetable) ✪ salt to taste
✪ 1 cup boiled, diced potatoes
✪ 3 rashers bacon.

METHOD:

Soak the peas overnight. Pressure-cook the next morning to a pulp, in 1 cup water for 10 minutes. Sieve the mixture. Heat oil in a pan on medium heat, cut the onion fine and sauté it till golden brown. To this add the sieved pea pulp, and the soup cubes diluted in the water, and salt. Stir cook for 10 minutes then add the diced potatoes. Cook for another 2 minutes. Remove. Serve with the bacon which had been fried crisply, then crushed and sprinkled over the soup in individual bowls.

Serves 8   Preparation Time : 20 minutes   Cooking Time : 20 minutes

Sopa de Ostras e Camarào

YOU NEED:

○ 4 chicken soup cubes ○ 4 cups warm water
○ 1 tablespoon butter ○ 1 tablespoon flour
○ salt and pepper to taste ○ 1 cup cleaned and deveined oysters
○ ½ cup cleaned, deveined prawns
○ 8 slices thin toasted bread
○ A few parsley or mint sprigs for garnishing

METHOD:

Dissolve the chicken cubes in the water. Keep aside. Heat butter in a pan on medium heat and stir fry the flour in it gradually, till it is a light brown colour. Now add the water with the cubes dissolved in it. Stir cook till thoroughly mixed. Now add the salt and pepper to taste, oysters and prawns. Simmer on a low flame for 10 minutes. Remove. Serve with the parsley or mint cut fine, and the toasted bread.

Serves : 8   *Preparation Time* : **15 minutes**   *Cooking Time* : **20 minutes**

Sopa de Camarão

YOU NEED:

○ 1 cup cleaned, deveined prawns
○ 2 cups water ○ 1 tablespoon cornflour
○ 1 cup chicken stock ○ 1 tablespoon oil
○ 1 large onion, chopped fine ○ 4 cloves garlic, chopped fine.
○ 1 large tomato chopped fine ○ 1 teaspoon grated cheddar cheese.

METHOD:

Boil the prawns in the 2 cups of water. Drain the prawns and keep the water aside. Chop the prawns fine. Dissolve cornflour in chicken stock and keep aside. Heat oil on medium flame and saute onion, garlic and tomato, till a thick paste is obtained. Stir-fry constantly. Add the 2 cups of reserved water and the cup of chicken stock. Stir cook, adding the prawns and grated cheese. Simmer on a low flame for 5 minutes.

Serves : 6   *Preparation Time* : **15 minutes**   *Cooking Time* : **15 minutes**

Aids to Goan Cooking

The requisites for authentic Goan cooking are certain ingredients peculiar to it. Hardly any Goan dish is complete without coconut as one of its main flavouring agents. Fresh coconut, in one form or the other, is added, either grated, ground fine into a paste or in the form of the milk, extracted from the flesh of the fresh coconut. These ripe coconuts are available in every open market in Goa and often in grocery stores too.

To obtain coconut milk, the coconut had to be pried into halves. Each half is then grated with a grater or scraper. The grated coconut flesh is then put into a blender or grinder, with enough water. The blender or grinder is worked at high speed, and then the contents removed and sieved through a fine sieve. The extract is the coconut milk specified in certain recipes. Canned, frozen or dessicated coconut can also be substituted under the directions given.

For most Goan fish and meat dishes, red, dried chillies/peppers are used. The Goan native chilli/pepper is large and pungent. It gives a red colour to the cooking without the fierce pungency of the normal Indian chilli/pepper. Since the Goa chilli/pepper is not always easy to obtain, the Kashmiri chilli/pepper in used instead. It has the same qualities as the Goan red, dried chilli/pepper. These red, dried chillies/peppers form the major ingredient for the ground spices in most fish and meat dishes. To help the busy housewife, it is a good idea to make and bottle certain spices for future use, keeping them in the refrigerator. See recipes for the 3 different ground spices, used as needed, on page nos.35-36.

Coconut Milk

For 1 cup coconut milk,
You Need:
❂ 1 cup (tightly packed) grated coconut ❂ 1 cup warm water

METHOD:
Put the coconut with ¾ of the cup of water into the blender/grinder for 1 minute at high speed. Remove the contents and put through a fine sieve. Squeeze out every drop of milk. Put the squeezed out pulp back into the blender/grinder with ¼ cup of water and work the blender/grinder for 30 seconds at high speed. Remove and squeeze out the remaining milk, adding it to the milk already extracted.

Tamarind Pulp

Tamarind is used as a souring agent in certain dishes. Otherwise, vinegar made from toddy, called 'Goa vinegar' is much prized. To use tamarind, one has to use only the pulp of the dried fruit.

You Need:
❂ 1 cup dried tamarind (tightly packed) ❂ 2 cups hot water
❂ 1 teaspoon salt ❂ 1 tablespoon sugar

METHOD:
Soak the tamarind in the water for 2 hours. Mix it by hand to a pulpy mass. Now put this mixture through a fine sieve, adding the salt and sugar to the sieved mixture. Add another tablespoon of hot water, if necessary, while sieving the tamarind pulp. Store in a jar in the refrigerator for use when needed.

1. Garlic-Ginger Paste

You Need:
- 100 gms. peeled garlic cloves
- 25 gms peeled ginger
- 1 tablespoon vinegar

METHOD:
Cut garlic and ginger fine. Put all the ingredients into the blender/grinder, and make into a fine paste. Bottle and refrigerate.

2. Recheiado Masala (sometimes called red masala)

You Need:
- 40 red, dried chillies/ peppers
- 20 (fat) cloves garlic
- 3" piece ginger
- 1 dessertspoon cummin seeds
- 1 dessertspoon peppercorns
- 20 cloves
- 4" piece cinnamon
- 1 teaspoon turmeric powder
- 1 dessertspoon sugar
- 1 teaspoon salt
- ¾ cup vinegar

METHOD:
Remove stems of chillies/peppers and cut them into small pieces.

Clean and cut fine the garlic and ginger. Put all the ingredients into the blender/grinder and make into a fine paste. Use a little more vinegar if necessary. The paste should be thick. Bottle and refrigerate.

N.B. This is the basic masala for Vindaloo, Balchao and Fish Recheiado. Use as needed in the proportions specified, adding whatever extras are needed.

3. Green Masala

You Need:

✪ 250 gms green chillies/peppers ✪ 2 full pods garlic
✪ 4" piece of ginger ✪ 1 tablespoon coriander seeds
✪ 1 dessertspoon cummin seeds ✪ 1 dessertspoon peppercorns
✪ 15 cloves ✪ 3" piece of cinnamon
✪ ½ cup chopped onions ✪ 3 cups fresh coriander leaves (tightly packed)
✪ 1 dessertspoon sugar ✪ salt to taste (about 1 teaspoon)
✪ 1½ cups vinegar, 1 level tablespoon turmeric powder

METHOD:

Wash and pat dry the chillies/peppers. Chop into pieces after removing the stalks. Clean the garlic and ginger and chop fine. Put all the ingredients into the blender/grinder and make into a paste. Bottle and refrigerate. Do the grinding in 2 lots.

N.B. this masala is used in some meat dishes as also to stuff mackerels/king fish/pomphrets etc, before frying. Very useful if one wishes to cook a spicy vegetable dish with beans, potatoes etc.

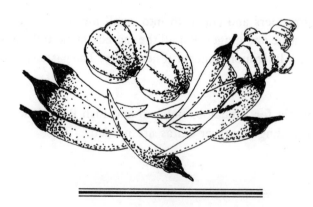

Fish

Fish is considered 'The Fruit of the Sea', and as such, the staple diet of the Goan is the well known meal of 'rice and fish curry'. All along the coastline of Goa, fishing trawlers can be seen casting their nets to collect the bounty of the Arabian Sea. The catch usually consists of king fish, mackerels, sardines, sharkfish, squid, sting rays, other small fish of many varieties, and then the lower sea fish, which includes prawns of all sizes, crabs, mussels, oysters and crayfish. The promphret, sometimes called plaice, is not a common find, hence the high price. During low tide, the smaller shell fish are collected, usually by the wife and children of the fisherman, and sold in the market. During the monsoon, from mid June till end September, fresh fish is scarce and sold at a premium price. People have to be satisfied with the fish caught in the rivers and creeks of Goa. During this season salted shrimp and mackerels prepared in many different ways, find their way to the family table.

Traditional Fish Curry

YOU NEED:

- 1 cup prawns (peeled deveined) or 6 slices fish
- salt to taste ○ 4 green chillies or peppers, deseeded
- 1 medium onion, sliced ○ 2 cups grated coconut (tightly packed)
- 1 tablespoon coriander seeds ○ ½ teaspoon cummin seeds
- 6 cloves garlic ○ 8 red, dried chillies or peppers
- 4 pepper corns ○ ½" piece ginger ○ ½ teaspoon turmeric powder
- 1 tablespoon tamarind pulp
- 3 cups warm water

METHOD:

Wash, clean and pat dry prawns or fish. Mix it with the salt, chillies or peppers and onion. Keep aside. Combine all the rest of the ingredients, except the tamarind pulp, and make into 2 lots, — putting each lot into the blender or grinder in turn, and extracting the spiced coconut milk by putting it through a fine sieve. When you have squeezed out every drop of liquid from the ground coconut mixture, add another ½ cup of warm water to the coconut mixture and put it into the blender or grinder once more, then through the sieve, so that all the milk has been extracted. Now put the coconut extract into a deep pan on a medium heat and stir cook for 30 minutes, till the sauce becomes thick. Add the marinated prawns or fish and the tamarind pulp to the boiling sauce. Stir cook, adding more salt if necessary. When the fish curry is reduced to half its quantity, remove the curry and put into a serving dish.

Serves : 6   *Preparation Time* : 20 minutes   *Cooking Time* : 30 minutes

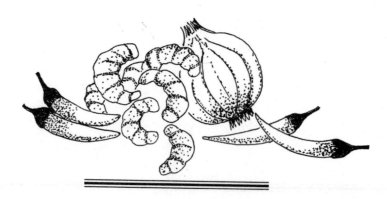

Sorak

Sorak is a curry made without fish, popular in the monsoon weather when fish is scarce. It goes well with a variety of pickles and/or salt-fish prepared in the Goan inimitable style. Eggs, hardboiled and then cut in halves horizontally, can be used to garnish the *sorak*.

YOU NEED:

○ 2 cups grated coconut ○ 1 tablespoon coriander seeds
○ ½ teaspoon cummin seeds ○ 4 cloves garlic
○ ¼ teaspoon turmeric powder
○ 4 red dried chillies or peppers
○ 1 large onion, halved and sliced
○ 4 green chillies or peppers, deseeded ○ 2 cups water
○ 1 dessertspoon tamarind pulp

METHOD:

Put the coconut with the spices and garlic into the blender or grinder with 2 cups water. Make into a fine paste. Put this coconut paste into a deep pan on medium heat and stir cook for 10 minutes. Then add the rest of the ingredients--the onion, chillies and tamarind--with the remaining cup of water. Let this boil and stir cook till the sorak is creamy. Remove.

N.B. If tamarind is not available, then substitutes include: a small green mango (sliced), a few *bimlis* (a vegetable which resembles the gherkin), a raw cooking apple or 1 tablespoon lemon juice.

Serves : 6   *Preparation Time* : **15 minutes**   *Cooking Time* : **30 minutes**

Onion Fish Curry

YOU NEED:

❂ ½ kg of any fish or prawns ❂ 1 cup coconut, grated
❂ 4 red, dried chillies or peppers
❂ ½ teaspoon peppercorns ❂ 6 cloves garlic
❂ 2 cups onion, chopped fine ❂ ½ teaspoon turmeric powder
❂ 1 tablespoon oil ❂ salt to taste

METHOD:

Clean fish, apply salt and keep aside. Grind to a fine paste the coconut, chillies or peppers, peppercorns, garlic and 1 cup onions. Add the turmeric powder to this mixture. Heat oil on a medium flame and saute 1 cup onions till golden brown in colour. Add the coconut ground with the spices. Stir fry for 2 minutes. Add gradually 2 cups water and allow the sauce to simmer on a low flame for 5 minutes. Continue stir cooking, and when sauce is reduced to half its original quantity, add the fish, salt to taste. Simmer till done.

Serves : 6   *Preparation Time* : **15 minutes**   *Cooking Time* : **20 minutes.**

Amotik: Fish curry (sour and hot)

YOU NEED:

❂ ½ kg shark fish or sting ray ❂ salt to taste
❂ 8 red dried red chillies or peppers ❂ 8 cloves garlic
❂ 1" piece ginger ❂ 10 peppercorns ❂ 8 cloves
❂ 1" stick of cinnamon ❂ 1 teaspoon cummin seeds
❂ ¼ teaspoon turmeric powder ❂ 1 teaspoon sugar
❂ 2 tablespoons vinegar ❂ 1 tablespoon oil
❂ 1 medium onion, chopped fine ❂ A few curry leaves ❂ 1½ cups water

METHOD:

Clean, wash and slice fish. Apply salt and keep aside. Grind all the spices garlic and ginger in the vinegar, adding the sugar. Heat oil on medium flame and saute onion a golden brown. Add the ground spices to this and stir fry for 1 minute. Add the curry leaves and the water gradually. Stir cook 15 minutes till the sauce is thick. Add the fish pieces and cook for a further 10 minutes. Remove and serve.

Serves 6   *Preparation Time* : **20 minutes**   *Cooking Time* : **25 minutes**

Crab Curry

You Need:

- 6 large crabs, boiled & cleaned (only body & claws used)
- 8 red dries chillies or Peppers ❂ 1 teaspoon cummin seeds
- ¼ teaspoon turmeric powder ❂ 8 cloves garlic ❂ ½" piece ginger
- 1 tablespoon oil ❂ 1 large onion sliced ❂ 2 tablespoons coconut, grated
- ¼ teaspoon garam masala ❂ 1 cup water ❂ 1 tablespoon tamarind pulp

Method:

Grind spices to a paste. Heat oil on a medium flame in a pan and saute sliced onion. Stir fry for 1 minute. Add ground spices and stir-fry for another minute. Add the coconut, tamarind, salt to taste and crabs. Simmer on a low flame, covered for 15 minutes. Stir-cook and add a little more water if necessary.

N.B. The crab claws can be lightly cracked and each body cut in halves, to felicitate eating.

Serves 8   Preparation Time : 20 minutes   Cooking Time : 20 minutes

Oyster Pie

You Need:

- 2 tablespoons butter ❂ 2 medium onions, chopped fine
- 2 medium tomatoes, chopped fine ❂ 4 cloves garlic, chopped fine
- 2 green chillies, deseeded, chopped fine ❂ salt and pepper to taste
- 2 tablespoons flour ❂ 1½ cups milk ❂ 1 cups cleaned oysters ❂ 2 eggs
- 2 soup cubes, chicken/vegetable ❂ ½ cup green peas, boiled
- 1 tablespoon cheese, grated ❂ 1 tablespoon breadcrumbs

Method:

Heat butter in a pan on medium flame. Sauté onions, tomatoes, garlic, chillies to a light brown. Add salt and pepper and the flour gradually, stirring all the time till a smooth consistency is acquired. Add the milk gradually and stir cook. Now add the oysters and stir cook for a further 5 minutes. Remove and cool.

Into this mixture add the 2 eggs, crumbled soup cubes and peas. Set oven at 375°F. Grease a baking dish and put in the cooked mixture. Sprinkle with bread crumbs and cheese. Bake for 30 minutes till golden brown on top. Serve with a green salad.

Serves 6   Preparation Time : 20 minutes   Cooking Time : 50 minutes.

Fried Fish Fingers/Shellfish Platter

You Need:

○ 4 fish fillets ○ 12 large prawns
○ 12 large oysters ○ 12 mussels
○ Juice of 2 lemons
○ salt and pepper to taste ○ ½ cup breadcrumbs
○ 2 eggs, beaten slightly. ○ ½ cup oil
○ 1 lemon for garnish

METHOD:

Pat dry the fish fillets, and cut into fingers. Shell, devein prawns, wash and pat dry. The oysters and mussels are also to be shelled, cleaned and washed. Pat dry. Marinate all the fish in the lemon juice, adding the salt and pepper. Heat the oil in a pan on medium flame, fry first the fish fingers, then the oysters, prawns and lastly the mussels. After dipping them in the beaten egg and then rolling them in the breadcrumbs. Serve on a platter, garnished with the lemon cut in thin slices.

Serves : 6   *Preparation Time* : **20 minutes**   *Cooking Time* : **25 minutes**

Fish Temperade

This recipe is specially for shellfish, crabs, prawns, mussels, clams etc. Failing this, sliced fish can be an adequate alternative.

You Need:

- ✪ 6 slices of any fish/1 cup shell fish, cleaned
- ✪ 1 tablespoon oil ✪ 3 red dries chillies/peppers
- ✪ 1 tablespoon coriander seeds ✪ 1 teaspoon cummin seeds
- ✪ 1 cup grated coconut ✪ 2 large onions, chopped fine
- ✪ ½ teaspoon turmeric powder ✪ 1 teaspoon sugar
- ✪ 6 cloves garlic, chopped fine ✪ ½" ginger, chopped fine
- ✪ 3 tablespoons tamarind pulp

Method:

Heat oil on medium flame, saute chillies, coriander, and cummin seeds till they pop. Remove from heat. Grind to a fine paste the coconut, ½ the onion, garlic and ginger. Heat the oil and saute the ground paste of coconut and spices. Stir fry for 1 minute, adding 1 cup water. Stir cook. Add Tamarind pulp, sugar, turmeric, and salt to taste. Stir cook for a further 2 minutes. Lastly add the shellfish fish. Simmer on a low flame, adding a little more water. Remove when the sauce is thick.

Serves : 4   *Preparation Time* : 30 minutes   *Cooking Time* : 20 minutes

Fish Recheiado

YOU NEED:
✪ 6 Mackerels ✪ Juice of 1 lemon
✪ Salt to taste ✪ ¼ teaspoon turmeric ✪ Oil for frying.

METHOD:
Clean fish, pat dry. Make a slit with a sharp knife on either side of the spine. Rub the salt, lemon juice and turmeric powder inside and outside the fish. Keep aside.

GRIND TO A FINE PASTE:
YOU NEED
✪ 8 red dried chillies/peppers
✪ ½ teaspoon cummin seeds ✪ 8 cloves garlic ✪ 10 peppercorns
✪ 1" piece ginger ✪ 8 cloves ✪ 1" piece cinnamon... in 2 tablespoons vinegar
✪ add salt to taste & ½ teaspoon sugar to this paste

METHOD:
Apply the ground spices inside the slits of the fish.
Secure with toothpicks. Heat oil on a medium flame and fry fish.

Serves : 6   Preparation Time : 30 minutes   Cooking Time : 15 minutes

Prawn Temperado

YOU NEED:
✪ 1 tablespoon oil ✪ 12 large prawns, deveined
✪ 250 gms white pumpkin, diced ✪ 4 red chillies, ground fine
✪ 1" ginger, chopped fine ✪ 1 cup thick coconut milk ✪ 4 green chillies, split
✪ ¼ teaspoon turmeric powder ✪ salt to taste

METHOD:
In a pan, on medium flame heat the oil. Stir-fry the prawns. Now add the rest of the ingredients and stir cook till the sauce is thick. About 20 minutes.
Serve with a squeeze of lemon juice. This dish is best eaten with plain white rice.

Serves : 4   Preparation Time : 15 minutes   Cooking Time : 25 minutes

Fish Balchão

YOU NEED:

○ 1 kg. fish fillets/1 kg large prawns, deveined
○ salt to taste ○ 10 cloves garlic,
○ ½ teaspoon turmeric powder ○ 1" piece ginger
○ 10 red dries chillies/peppers ○ ¼ teaspoon cumin seeds
○ ¼ teaspoon mustard seeds ○ 1 teaspoon sugar
○ 1 dessertspoon dried shrimps, powdered ○ 3 tablespoons oil
○ 4 medium onions, chopped fine ○ 6 tablespoons tomato puree.

METHOD:
Clean fish prawns and pat dry. Apply salt and turmeric. Keep aside. Grind garlic, ginger and spices in 2 tablespoons vinegar, adding sugar and the dried shirmps. Heat oil in a frying pan. Fry the fish lightly on both sides to a golden brown. Remove the fish slices/prawns carefully. Keep aside. In the same pan but in the oil, adding another tablespoon necessary, saute the onions and add the tomato puree. Stir cook for 2 minutes. Now add the spices ground in vinegar and stir cook for a further 5 minutes. Place the fish fillets/prawns carefully in the prepared sauce and on a low flame, cook the fish for 2 minutes, shaking the pan gently occasionally. Serve garnished with chopped coriander leaves

Serves : 8   *Preparation Time* : **30 minutes**   *Cooking Time* : **15 minutes**

N.B. This preparation can be kept for 3 to 4 days without losing its flavour. It can also be prepared beforehand and heated gently before serving. If dried shrimps are not available, use I tablespoon finely ground fresh prawns instead.

Langouste Balchão

In Goa the fishermen usually get a catch of big cray-fish, called langouste sometimes mistaken of the lobster. In fact, it is often called lobster on a menu, and priced accordingly!

You Need:

✪ 6 cray fish ✪ 2 tablespoons oil.

✪ 2 medium onions, chopped fine ✪ 2 green chillies, chopped fine

✪ 2 medium tomatoes, chopped fine

✪ 2 level tablespoons recheiado masala (see introductory section)

✪ 1 tablespoon dried shrimps, powdered ✪ 1 teaspoon sugar

✪ salt to taste

Method:

Wash the cray-fish and then put into a pot of boiling water for 1 minute. The shell will turn pinkish orange. Drain. Cool. Since most of the meat is in the tail, cut each tail into 2 equal pieces. Keep the cray fish heads for decoration. With a sharp knife cut down the centre underside of the cray-fish tails and extract the meat carefully, keeping the tail shells aside. Devein the meat and cut into small pieces. Keep aside.

Heat the oil in a pan on medium heat. Saute the onions, green chillies/peppers, and tomatoes, till it is reduced to a thick paste. Now add the recheiado masala and lower the heat. Stir fry for 1 minute, add the cried shrimp powder, sugar, salt and cray-fish. Stir fry and test for salt, adding more if necessary. Cook for another 2 minutes. Remove from heat and cool. To serve, fill each half of the tails with the cray-fish balchao. Arrange on a flat serving dish, the 6 complete cray-fish, that is:2 tail parts and a head. Serve with a fresh green salad.

Serves 6 *Preparation Time* : 30 minutes   *Cooking Time* : 15 minutes.

Portuguese Sardines

YOU NEED:

○ 12 large sardines ○   ¾ cup olive oil
○   ½ cup tomato puree ○ 1 teaspoon peppercorns
○ 8 cloves garlic, chopped fine ○ salt to taste
○   ½ teaspoon sugar ○ 1 tablespoon vinegar ○   1/3 cup water

METHOD:

Wash, clean and pat dry the fish. Rub salt inside and outside each fish. Place sardines in a pressure cooker. Mix the olive oil, tomato puree, peppercorns, garlic, salt, sugar, vinegar and water together. Pour over the fish. Pressure cook for 10 minutes. Remove.

Serves : 6   *Preparation Time* : **15 minutes**   *Cooking Time* : **10 minutes**

Fofos de Peixe

YOU NEED:

○   ½ Kg fish, cleaned ○ salt to taste
○ 6 pepper corns ○ 1 cup water
○ 1 large potato boiled, mashed ○ 2 eggs
○ 4 cloves garlic, chopped fine
○   ½" piece ginger, chopped fine
○ 3 green chillies/peppers, chopped fine ○ Juice of 1 lemon
○ 1 onion, chopped fine ○ small sprig coriander, chopped fine
○ cup breadcrumbs ○ oil for frying.

METHOD:

Put the cleaned fish in a pan on medium heat, with the pepper corns 1 cup water and salt to taste, to boil, till all the water has been absorbed. Remove skin and debone the fish. With a fork, mash the boiled fish and potato and combine with 1 egg, garlic, ginger, chillies/peppers lemon juice, coriander and onion. Form into flat, oval cutlets. Dip each Fogos in the remaining beaten egg, then roll in breadcrumbs. Heat oil in a frying pan on medium heat, and fry the cutlets till they are a golden brown on each side. Makes 1 dozen cutlets.

Preparation Time : **30 minutes**   *Cooking Time* : **15 minutes**

N.B. This recipe can be used for ½ kg prawns instead of ½ kg fish.

Caldeirada

YOU NEED:

✪ 6 slices of fish/12 large prawns ✪ salt to taste
✪ 2 cups water ✪ 2 cups coconut, grated ✪ 1 tablespoon coriander
✪ ½ teaspoon cumin seeds ✪ 6 cloves garlic ✪ ½" piece ginger
✪ 2 medium onions sliced ✪ 1 large tomato, sliced.
✪ 4 green chillies/peppers ✪ a dash of lemon juice.

METHOD:

Clean fish/devein and clean prawns, apply salt keep aside. In the blender/grinder put the grated coconut, coriander, cumin, garlic and ginger with 2 cups of water, till a fine paste is obtained. Put this mixture through a fine sieve and extract all the spiced coconut milk. Put a deep pan on medium flame and put in the coconut extract, green chillies, onions and tomatoes. Stir cook till the coconut milk extract is creamy. Add the fish/prawns and salt to taste with a dash of the lemon juice.

This dish is versatile, as you may cook with only fish or only prawns, or with a mixture of prawns, oysters and mussels using the same method.

Serves : 6   *Preparation Time* : **20 minutes**   *Cooking Time* : **20 minutes**

Fish Guisado

YOU NEED:

✪ 2 tablespoons oil ✪ 2 large onions, sliced
✪ 6 cloves garlic ✪ ½" piece ginger ✪ 5 green, chillies, deseeded
✪ 2 large tomatoes, sliced ✪ ¼ teaspoon turmeric powder
✪ 1 dessertspoon vinegar ✪ ¼ teaspoon sugar ✪ salt and pepper to taste
✪ ½ cup water ✪ 1 kg sliced fish/ fillets

METHOD:

Heat oil in a pan on medium flame and saute onions till golden brown. Add garlic, ginger , greenchillies, tomatoes, turmeric, vinegar sugar, salt, pepper and water. Stir cook till it is a thick sauce. Add the fish with ½ cup water and salt and pepper to taste, and cook gently. Shaking the pan occasionally, for another 10 minutes. Serve garnished with a fresh sprig of coriander leaves.

N.B. Usually, all fish dishes when served are accompanied with a fresh salad, or a platter of boiled vegetables... okra, french beans, cauliflower, cabbage, sliced tomatoes and onions.

Serves 6   Preparation Time : **20 minutes**   *Cooking Time* : **20 minutes**

Fish Recheiado

Fotos de Riera

Soup: Caldo de Verde

Pickles – Mango, Tendli and Brinjal

Apa de Camarão

Sorpotel and Sannas

Prawn Curry and Rice with Accompaniments

Coconut-Chicken Curry

Bibinca

Sans Rival

Starters: Croquettes, Rissóis de Camarão and King Prawns

Sans Rival

A Letria

Baked Crabs and Mussels in Shell

Dedos de Damas ───→

Feijoada with Puris

Apa de Camarão

You Need:

⊘ 2 cups rice ⊘ 1½ cups grated coconut ⊘ 1½ cups toddy ⊘ 350 gms. sugar
⊘ salt to taste ⊘ 6 eggs ⊘ 1 cup prawn balchao ⊘ 1 tablespoon butter

METHOD:

Wash and soak rice over night. Next morning grind rice and coconut separately in a blender/grinder, using the toddy, to make a fine batter. Add the salt and sugar and keep aside for 3 to 4 hours till the batter is well risen. Now beat gently together the 6 egg yolks and 3 of the egg whites only. Add the beaten eggs to the rice-coconut mixture. Meanwhile line a cake tin, 8" in diameter with greased butter paper. Divide the rice coconut mixture into two portions. Put one portion at the bottom of the cake tin evenly. Now spread the Prawn Balchao (see recipe on Page 79) carefully over this bottom layer, and then spread the remaining portion over the Prawn Balchao mixture. Set the oven at 375 F., and when it is hot (appx.10 mins.) put in the Apa de Camarao and bake in the middle of the oven till it is risen and the top is golden brown in colour. Remove. Cool and serve either as a starter or a snack with drinks.

Serves : 12. Preparation Time : 40 minutes. Cooking Time : 20 minutes.

N.B. For the Prawn Balchao follow the same recipe for fish balchao but using only prawns. It is worthwhile making some Prawn Balchao and keeping it in the refrigerator for future use. It is what I usually do.

Fish Moile

You Need

⊘ 8 slices fish/prawns ⊘ 1 coconut, grated
⊘ 1 tablespoon oil ⊘ 2 medium onions, sliced ⊘ 2 medium tomatoes, quartered
⊘ 4 green chillies, deseeded ⊘ 6 cloves garlic, chopped fine
⊘ 1" fresh ginger, chopped fine ⊘ ¼ teaspoon turmeric powder ⊘ salt to taste

METHOD:

Pat dry the fish, apply salt and keep aside. Extract 1½ cups coconut milk by putting the grated coconut in the blender/grinder with 1½ cups water. Heat oil in a pan on medium heat, and saute onion. Add the rest of the ingredients, except fish. Let the sauce simmer on low heat till it is thick (apprx. 15 mins.). Add the fish carefully and cook for further 7 minutes, shaking the pan occasionally.

Serves 6   Preparation Time : 15 minutes   Cooking Time : 28 minutes

Vegetarian Favourites

These are some of the most popular vegetarian dishes, enjoyed by all and prepared on special occasions. Dried beans, lentils and vegetables are grown in the rice fields after the harvest is collected. The rice fields then present a pretty picture patches of red and green spinach beans, spring onions and okra. Most of the vegetables are cooked with grated coconut, and some with a sprinkling of tiny prawns. The section also includes some recipes for rice bread, rice muffins and popular pulaos.

Feijoada

YOU NEED:

✪ 1 cup dried black-eyed beans ✪ 2 tablespoons oil
✪ 2 onion, chopped fine ✪ 2 tomatoes chopped fine
✪ 6 cloves garlic ✪ 1" piece ginger made into a paste
✪ ¼ teaspoon turmeric powder ✪ 1 tablespoon tamarind pulp
✪ ¼ teaspoon chilli powder/paprika powder
✪ 1 teaspoon sugar ✪ salt to taste
✪ 1 cup coconut milk

METHOD:

Soak beans over night. The next morning throw out the old water and pressure cook with 1 cup fresh water.

Heat oil in a pan and saute onion, tomatoes and garlic-ginger paste, till golden brown. Add turmeric powder, tamarind pulp, chilli/paprika powder, sugar, salt to taste, coconut milk and beans. Simmer on low flame for 15 minutes, till a thick sauce is obtained.

Serves 6   **Preparation Time : 20 minutes**   **Cooking Time : 30 minutes**

Kokum Curry (Binda Fruit)

YOU NEED:

✪ ½ coconut, grated ✪ 3 green chillies
✪ 6 gloves garlic ✪ Pinch of asafoetida ✪ salt to taste
✪ ½ cup warm water ✪ 8 dried kokum peels.

METHOD:

Grind the coconut, chillies and garlic together, and extract the coconut milk. Add the asafoetida and salt to the coconut milk extract. Soak the kokum peel and the residue of the coconut milk extract in the ½ cup warm water. Keep aside for 15 minutes, then extract the juice. Mix with the above coconut milk extract

You may add a few cut corriander leaves and ½ teaspoon of sugar for added flavour.

Serves : 4   *Preparation Time : 15 minutes*

Sprouted Lentil Curry

You Need:

○ 2 cups sprouted, green lentils (moong)
○ 1 cup water ○ 1 cup grated coconut ○ 8 peppercorns
○ 1" piece cinnamon ○ 6 cloves ○ 8 cloves garlic ○ 2 tablespoons oil
○ ½ teaspoon mustard seeds ○ a few curry leaves
○ 1 medium onion, chopped fine ○ 1/3 cup peanuts ○ 1 dessertspoon tamarind pulp
○ 1½ cups water ○ 1 teaspoon sugar ○ salt to taste

METHOD:

Wash and in the one cup water, boil the sprouted green lentils in a pan on medium heat, for 5 minutes. Grind into a fine paste in the blender/grinder the coconut, peppercorns, cinnamon, cloves, and garlic. Heat the oil in a pan on medium heat saute the mustard seeds and curry leaves for ½ minute. Add the onion and stir fry till they are browned. Now add the ground coconut with spices and stir fry for 1 minute. Add the rest of the ingredients, including the stock of the boiled lentils and the additional 1½ cups water. Add salt. Stir cook till the sauce is thick. about 25 minutes. Remove.

Serves : 6   *Preparation Time* : 15 minutes   *Cooking Time* : 30 minutes.

Breadfruit Curry

You Need:

○ 1 large breadfruit (apprx. 350 gms.) ○ 2 cups water ○ 1 cup grated coconut
○ ½ cup onions, chopped fine ○ 6 dried red chillies/peppers
○ 1 tablespoon coriander seeds ○ ½ teaspoon cumin seeds
○ 6 cloves garlic chopped fine ○ 1" piece ginger, chopped fine
○ a few curry leaves ○ ¼ teaspoon turmeric powder ○ 1 dessertspoon sugar
○ salt to taste ○ 2 tablespoons tamarind pulp ○ 1½ cups water

METHOD:

Peel the breadfruit and cut into large cubes. Immerse in the 2 cups water. Keep aside. In a blender/ grinder, grind the coconut, half the onion and all the spices. Heat the oil in a deep pan on medium heat. Saute rest of the onion, garlic, ginger and curry leaves. Add the turmeric powder, sugar and salt to taste, then the ground spices. Stir fry for another minute, then add the tamarind pulp, and water breadfruit, after draining the breadfruit and throwing away the water it was immersed in. Stir cook gently for another 20 minutes till the sauce is thick and creamy.

Serves : 6   *Preparation Time* : 15 minutes   *Cooking Time* : 25 minutes

Pungent Feijoada

You Need
- 1½ cups fejoan (red kidney beans)
- 8 red dried peppers ○ 10 cloves ○ 1 teaspoon peppercorns
- 1 tablespoon coriander seeds ○ 1 teaspoon cumin seeds
- 1 cup coconut, grated 2 tablespoons oil
- 2 tablespoons oil ○ 2 larger onions, chopped fine
- 1 tablespoon tamarind pulp ○ salt to taste

METHOD:

Soak beans over night and pressure cook the next day in the water in which they were soaked. Roast all the spices with the grated coconut and grind fine in the blender/grinder. Heat oil in a pan, saute the onion in hot oil, add the roasted ground spices and stir fry for a minute. Then add the beans, salt to taste and tamarind pulp, with enough water to make a thick sauce. Stir cook for 10 minutes.

Serves : 8   *Preparation Time* : **15 minutes**   *Cooking Time* : **15 minutes**

This Fejoda goes well with the rice bread, whose recipe follows. Also included are recipes for Sannas, a steamed rice muffin.

Rice Bread

You Need:
- 200 gms. rice flour ○ ½ cup grated coconut
- 1 onion, chopped fine ○ a few sprigs coriander, chopped fine
- 1 teaspoon sugar ○ 2 green chillies/peppers, deseeded
- salt to taste ○ 2 tablespoons clarified butter (ghee)

METHOD:

Mix the rice flour with enough water to make a stiff dough. Add the coconut, onion, coriander, sugar and chillies/peppers, salt and water enough to make a soft and pliable dough. Keep aside for 2 hours. Grease a griddle/flat pan on medium heat. Roll out the dough (after making it into balls) on a floured board, and bake the bread on both sides, putting a little clarified butter/ghee on each side as you turn it.

Serves 6   *Preparation Time* : **15 minutes**   *Cooking Time* : **20 minutes**

Sannas

YOU NEED:

- 2 cups rice ✪ 1 coconut, grated
- ½ bottle toddy ✪ 1 tablespoon sugar
- salt to taste

METHOD:

Wash and soak rice overnight. In a blender/grinder, grind the rice and coconut separately, with the toddy, then mix all the ingredients together, using more toddy if needed to make a thick batter. Leave in a warm place for 4 hours till the mixture ferments and rises. Get the steaming vessel ready on medium flame with the required amount of water in it. Put a tablespoonful of the batter into each moulds and steam on medium heat till the sannas are fluffy and done right through. Makes about 20 sannas.

Preparation Time : **20 minutes**   *Cooking Time* : **45 minutes**

Sannas

This recipe is for those who are unable to get the required toddy. It is very successful and done just as fast.

YOU NEED:

- 2 cups boiled rice ✪ 2 cups raw rice
- ¾ cup split white lentils (urad) ✪ 1 dessertspoon dry yeast
- 1 teaspoon sugar ✪ 1 cup coconut milk
- salt to taste

METHOD:

Wash and soak each of the first 3 ingredients overnight, separately. Next morning put the dry yeast in a bowl with the sugar and 3 tablespoons warm water. When it is bubbly and rises, add it to the rice (both kinds) and the lentils which have been ground fine in the blender/grinder with the coconut milk. Add salt to taste and keep aside for 5 hours till it doubles in quantity. Get the steaming vessel ready on medium flame with the required amount of water in it. Put a tablespoonful of the batter into each of the moulds and steam on medium heat till the sannas are fiuffy and done right through. Makes about 36 sannas.

Preparation Time : **30 minutes**   *Cooking Time* : **40 minutes**

Pez (Congee)

YOU NEED:

✪ 1 cup Goa Rice (reddish in colour and thick grained)
✪ 4 cups water ✪ salt to taste

METHOD:

Clean and wash rice thoroughly. Put into a thick bottomed vessel along with the water and salt, and cook covered till the rice grains are soft. This will take approx. 40 minutes.

N.B. This preparation is eaten in the village homes of Goa usually at about 11 a.m., along with the water pickle, para, fish mole or 'KAL CHE KUDHI' (yesterdays prawn curry which had been cooked dry on a high heat along with a sliced onion.) it is absolutely delicious with any one or two of these accompaniments. This pez is also given to babies as their first solid food and to patients recouping from an illness.

Serves : 3   Preparation Time : 10 minutes   Cooking Time : 45 minutes

Arroz

YOU NEED:

✪ 3 cups Basmati Rice. ✪ 4 tablespoons ghee (clarified butter)
✪ 1 large onion, sliced ✪ 6 cloves ✪ 2 sticks cinnamon ✪ 4 whole cardamoms
✪ 5 cups chicken stock + 1 teaspoon fresh lemon juice.
✪ salt to taste ✪ 1 cup shredded chicken meat (boiled)*
✪ a few cocktail sausages* ✪ a handful of olives

METHOD:

Wash rice thoroughly. In a thick bottomed vessel, heat the ghee on a medium flame. Saute sliced onion to a golden brown. Add the spices and stir fry for 2 minutes. Add the rice and stir fry for 1 minute. Add the chicken stock with the lemon juice and salt to taste. Close the vessel with its lid and on a low flame let the Arroz simmer till all the liquid has been absorbed and the Arroz is light and fluffy. Serve hot, decorated with the shredded chicken, cocktail sausages and olives.

N.B. You may dissolve 2 chicken soup cubes in the chicken stock for a stronger flavour.

Serves : 8   Preparation time : 25 minutes   Cooking time : 25 minutes.

---

* Vegetarians may eliminate the sausages and cup of shredded chicken and chicken cubes. Vegetable stock, green peas and vegetarian cup cubes can be alternatively used.

Coconut Pullao

YOU NEED:

- 3 cups Basmati Rice
- 1 tablespoons ghee (clarified butter)
- 1 large onion, sliced ❂ 6 cloves
- 2 sticks cinnamon ❂ 4 whole cardamoms
- 2 cups thick coconut milk
- 3 cups water ❂ 1 teaspoon fresh lemon juice.
- salt to taste ❂ ½ cup green peas, boiled
- 2 cups cauliflower flowerets boiled
- 1 tablespoon cashew nuts, fried lightly

METHOD:

Wash rice thoroughly. In a thick vessel, heat the ghee on medium flame and sauté the sliced onion to a golden brown. Add the spices and stir-fry for 2 minutes. Now add the rice and stir-fry for 1 minute. Add the coconut milk and water mixed together, with salt to taste, and a teaspoon of fresh lemon juice. Close the vessel with its lid, and on a low flame, let the Coconut/Pullao cook, for about 20 minutes till all the water has been absorbed and the rice is light and fluffy. Serve hot with the green peas, and cauliflower flowerets mixed with the pullao, and the cashew nuts on top for decoration.

Serves : 8   Preparation Time : 25 minutes   Cooking Time : 25 minutes

Coconut Pulao

For your

○ 1½ cups Basmati Rice
○ 4 tablespoons ghee (clarified butter)
○ 1 large onion, sliced thin, fried
○ 2 sticks cinnamon ○ 4 whole cardamom
○ 2 cups thick coconut milk
○ 4 cups water ○ 1 teaspoon fresh lemon juice
○ salt to taste ○ ½ cup green peas, boiled
○ ½ cups cauliflower florets, boiled
○ 1 tablespoon cashew nuts, fried lightly

Method

Wash rice thoroughly. In a thick-bottomed pan, heat the ghee on medium flame and fry the sliced onion to a golden brown. Add the spices and slowly fry 1-2 minutes. Now add the rice and stir fry for 2 minutes. Add the coconut milk and water mixed together, with salt to taste, and a tablespoon of fresh lemon juice. Cover the vessel with its lid and on low flame, let the Coconut milk cook for about 20 minutes till the water has been absorbed and the rice is light and fluffy. Serve hot with the green peas and cauliflower flowerets mixed with the pulao, and the cashew nuts on top for decoration.

Serves 4-6   Preparation Time : 15 minutes   Cooking Time   25 minutes

Meats

The urban Goan is a great meat and fish eater, with a preference for pork, chicken, beef and mutton in that order. For the usual 'fish curry and rice' on the table along with varying accompaniments. The evening meal usually consists of a meat dish with a salad or cooked vegetable, boiled or otherwise. Pork and chicken are generally cooked for special occasions and Sundays. Many of the ingredients used in Goan meat dishes are common for pork, beef, mutton and chicken. Of course 'sorpotel', a pork dish peculiar only to Goa, is the all time favourite. And many are the housewives who claim that **their** Sorpotel is the best! The nice thing about sorpotel is that it can be prepared at least 4 to 5 days in advance of the Special Day. It is warmed up once a day till the day it is served, and eaten, with the inimitable 'sanna' a steamed rice muffin. Here is a Goan song dedicated to 'sorpotel'.

SORPOTEL

'For the hotch potch known as Haggis
Let the Scotsman yearn or yell
For the taste of Yorkshire pudding
Let the English family dwell.

For the famed Tandoori Chicken
That Punjabis praise like hell
But for us who hail from Goa
There's nothing like Sorpotel!

From the bigwigs in Colaba
To the small fry in Cavel
From the growing tribes in Bandra
To the remnants in Parel.

From the lovely girls in Glaxo
To the boys in Burmah Shell
There's no Goan whose mouth won't water
When you talk of Sorpotel!

And Oh! for Christmas dinner
Don't you think it would be swell
If by some freak of fortune
Or by some magic spell

We could, as they have in Goa
A bottle of the cajel
And toddy leavened sannas
To go with Sorpotel!

Sorpotel

You Need:

- 1 kg boneless pork
- 1 pork liver, 1 heart, 1 tongue, 2 kidneys
- 3 cups water ○ 12 red dried chillies/peppers
- 12 peppercorns ○ 12 cloves garlic
- 1" piece ginger ○ 1 teaspoon cumin seeds
- 8 cloves ○ Two 1" pieces cinnamon
- ¾ cup vinegar ○ ½ cup oil
- 1 peg coconut feni ○ salt to taste
- 6 green chillies/peppers, chopped
- 4 medium onions, chopped fine

METHOD:

Wash and pat dry the meats. Put in a deep pan with the water on medium heat. Cover with a lid and parboil the meats, (approximately 20 minutes). Remove from the fire, cool and dice the meats fine. Keep aside the water. Put all the spices except the green chillies/peppers and onion, into the blender/grinder with the vinegar and grind to a fine paste. Heat the oil in a deep pan on medium heat and lightly fry all the diced meat, stir frying continuously till it is lightly browned. To this fried meat add the ground spices in vinegar and stir fry for 5 minutes. Add salt to taste, coconut feni, any remaining vinegar, the stock of the boiled meat, chopped onions and green chillies. Lower the heat and let the sorpotel simmer for 45 minutes of more. Take care to stir occasionally. When the oil comes to the top and the sauce is thick, remove from heat. Remember that sorpotel tastes better on the 3rd. or 4th day, after it has been warmed up once a day till the day it is served. It is customary to serve sorpotel with sannas for special occasions.

Serves 10   *Preparation Time* : 30 minutes   *Cooking Time* : 1 hour

Cabidela

This dish is prepared from the meat of a young pig/pigling

You Need:

○ 1 kg. meat ○ 1 pork liver, 1 heart, I tongue, 2 kidneys
○ 12 red dried chillies/peppers ○ 10 peppercorns
○ 10 cloves garlic ○ 1" piece of ginger ○ 1 teaspoon cumin seeds
○ 8 cloves ○ Two 1" pieces of cinnamon
○½ cup vinegar ○ ¼ cup oil ○ 1 cup water
○ 1/3 cup blood of pigling (optional)
○ 1 teaspoon sugar

Method:

Clean wash and pat dry the meat. Cut into small cubes. Apply salt to taste. Then grind all the spices, except the greenchillies/peppers and onion, in the blender/grinder to a fine paste in the vinegar. Apply this ground paste to the meat and keep aside for 2 hours. After 2 hours, heat the oil in a deep pan on medium heat and stir fry the spiced meat for 10 minutes. Now add the onions, chillies/peppers, feni, water and blood. Stir cook, adding the sugar and more salt if necessary. Lower the flame and stir cook for a further 25 minutes, till the cabidela should be prepared 3 to 4 days in advance and reheated once a day till it is ready to be served.

Serves : **10** *Preparation Time* : **25 minutes** *Cooking Time* : **45 minutes**

Tripas à Goesa (Tripe)

This dish is tedious to prepare and is an acquired taste. It is prepared from the small intestines and stomach of the pigling. In Goa, these are usually thoroughly cleaned and washed by the seller of pork meat. It is recommended however to repeat the process again at home.

YOU NEED:
○ The intestines and stomach of 1 pigling
○ 2 tablespoons salt ○ Water ○ 15 red dried chillies/peppers
○ 1 large pod garlic ○ 1" piece ginger ○ 1 teaspoon cumin seeds
○ 1 teaspoon peppercorns ○ 10 cloves ○ 2" piece cinnamon
○ 1 level teaspoon turmeric powder ○ 1¼ cups vinegar
○ ½ cup oil ○ 2 cups onion, chopped fine

METHOD:
Wash the tripe under running water thoroughly. Put it in a deep pan with enough water to cover the contents with 1 tablespoon salt and 1 tablespoon vinegar. Boil on high heat for 15 minutes. Drain the water and wash again thoroughly under running water. Cut into small pieces, add the remaining salt and keep aside. Grind all the spices, garlic and ginger in vinegar in the blender/grinder to a fine past. Heat the oil in a deep pan on medium heat. Saute the onion till it is a golden brown in colour. Add the ground paste and saute for 2 minutes. Add the tripe and 4 cups water. Stir cook on medium heat for 20 minutes. Then lower the heat and let the Tripas A Goesa simmer for another 30 minutes till the sauce is thick and the oil float to the top. Keep aside. Reheat the Tripas A Goesa once a day for the next 4 days, adding a little water each time and stir cooking all time. A teaspoon of sugar is often added, if preferred.

Serves : 10   *Preparation Time* : 40 minutes   *Cooking Time* : 1 hour

Pork Balchão

You Need:

- 1 kg. boneless pork ○ salt to taste
- 12 dried red chillies/peppers
- 10 peppercorns ○ 8 cloves
- 2" piece cinnamon ○ 1 teaspoon cumin seeds
- 10 cloves garlic ○ 1" piece ginger ○ ½ cup vinegar
- 1/3 cup oil ○ ½ cup chopped onion
- 4 cloves garlic ○ 1 tablespoon dried prawn powder
- 1 teaspoon sugar ○ 1½ cups water

METHOD:

Clean, wash and pat dry the pork. Cut into cubes and apply salt. In the blender/grinder; grind all the spices in vinegar, excepting the onion and 4 cloves garlic. Apply the ground spices to the meat and keep aside for 2 hours. After 2 hours, heat the oil in a deep pan on medium heat and stir-fry the marinated meat, for 15 minutes. Now add the rest of the ingredients. Stir-fry for a further 5 minutes. Add the water and more salt if necessary. Lower the heat and stir cook for 30 minutes till the pork balchao is cooked and the sauce thick. The oil will come to the top. This dish increases in flavour and enjoyment if it is prepared 3 to 4 days in advance, and reheated once a day before serving.

Serves **8**   *Preparation Time* **: 20 minutes**   *Cooking Time* **: 45 minutes**

Pork Baffado

You need:

✪ 1 kg. pork ✪   ½ kg. beef undercut ✪ 15 cloves garlic
✪ 1" piece ginger ✪ 15 peppercorns ✪ 10 cloves ✪ 2" piece cinnamon
✪ 1 teaspoon cumin seeds ✪   ½ teaspoon mustard seeds
✪ Small bunch fresh coriander ✪ 10 green chillies/peppers
✪ 4 tablespoons vinegar ✪ 1 lemon-sized ball tamarind ✪ 1 teaspoon sugar
✪ 250 gms. tiny whole onions, peeled✪ 4 tablespoons oil
✪ 250 gms. tiny potatoes, boiled and peeled ✪ 2 cups water

METHOD:

Clean and cut meats into small pieces. Apply salt and keep aside for ½ hour. Grind all the spices, garlic and ginger in vinegar, including the green chillies and fresh coriander. Extract tamarind pulp. Heat oil in a pan on medium heat and stir fry the ground spices for 2 minutes. Add sugar, meats stir cooking and adding the remaining vinegar, tamarind pulp and salt to taste. Lower flame, add potatoes, onions and gradually the 2 cups water, stirring occasionally. Cover the pan and allow to cook for ½ hour shaking the pan occasionally till the meat is soft and the oil comes to the top.

Serves : 8   Preparation Time : 35 minutes   Cooking Time : 35 minutes.

Pork Assado

You Need:

✪ 2 kgs. pork ✪ salt to taste 4 red dried chillies/peppers
✪ 6 green chillies/peppers ✪ ½ teaspoon cumin seeds ✪ 8 peppercorns
✪ 1" piece ginger ✪ 8 cloves garlic ✪ ¼ teaspoon turmeric powder
✪ 2 tablespoons oil ✪ 1 tablespoon tamarind extract ✪ 2 cups water
✪ 4 medium potatoes ✪ 4 medium onions, ✪ 1 large tomato, sliced

METHOD:

Clean meat, prick all over with a fork and apply salt and keep aside for ½ hour. Grind all the spices, garlic and ginger in a blender/grinder. Heat oil in a pan on medium flame and brown meat all over turning well till all sides are browned. Remove meat and saute ground spices. Add browned meat to the saute with the tamarind extract, onion, tomato, potatoes and 2 cups water. Simmer on a low flame with the pan covered, till the meat is soft. Slice the meat and potatoes before serving. This dish well with boiled french beans and carrots.

Serves : 12   Preparation Time : 30 minutes   Cooking Time : 40 minutes

Roast Pigling

You Need:

- One small pigling (apprx. 4 to 6 kgs.)
- 6 peppercorns ○ 2" piece ginger ○ 8 cloves garlic
- Juice of 2 lemons ○ salt to taste
- 2 tablespoons pork lard/dripping ○ 2 large onions, chopped fine
- 2 large tomatoes, chopped fine
- 4 green chillies/peppers, deseeded, chopped fine
- 6 cloves garlic, ○ ½ cup coriander
- some mint leaves, chopped fine ○ 1 cup breadcrumbs
- ½ cup green peas ○ 2 medium potatoes, boiled, diced

METHOD:

The pigling is bought cleaned, with the stomach slit, minus the hooves and body hair. Wash the pigling thoroughly and pat dry inside and outside, reserving the liver and kidneys. Wash the liver and kidneys and boil in ½ cup water and garlic and apply this marinated with the lemon/juice to the pigling inside and outside. Add salt to taste. Keep aside for 2 to 4 hours. Now prepare the stuffing. Heat the oil in a pan. Add the onions and tomatoes, green chillies, garlic and the herbs to this. Saute to a light brown colour, stir frying all the time. To this add the breadcrumbs, peas and potatoes and salt to taste. Stir cook till the stuffing is well cooked (apprx. 10 mins.). Lay the pigling flat on its back and fill the inside with this stuffing. Secure the stuffing by sewing the slit stomach together. Turn oven to 400° F, and arrange the pigling on a baking/ roasting tray. Apply the lard/dripping and place the tray in the middle of the oven. After 45 minutes, very carefully turn the pigling over and apply more fat to it. Leave for another 40 minutes. When the skin turns crackling' crisp, switch off the oven and serve.

Serves : 12   *Preparation Time* : 40 minutes   *Cooking Time* : 1½ hours

Note: Roast pigling is served on a big/flat platter with a small apple in the mouth of the pigling and a few small roasted potatoes around.

Pork Vindaloo

YOU NEED:

○ 1 kg, lean pork, cleaned ○ salt to taste ○ 10 red dried chillies/peppers
○ 10 peppercorns ○ 10 cloves garlic ○ I" piece ginger ○ 8 cloves
○ 1" piece cinnamon ○ 1 teaspoon cumin seeds ○ ½ teaspoon mustard seeds
○ ½ teaspoon sugar ○ ½ cup vinegar ○ 2 tablespoons oil
○ ½ peg coconut feni ○ 2 medium onions, chopped fine ○ 2 cups water

METHOD:

Cut the cleaned pork into bite-sized pieces. Apply salt and keep aside. Grind all the spices in the vinegar, adding the ½ teaspoon sugar. Apply the ground spices to the meat and keep aside for 4 hours. Heat the oil in a pan on medium heat and add the meat. Stir fry the meat for 5 minutes, then add the chopped onion, coconut feni, rest of the vinegar and the water gradually. Cover the pan and lower heat. Stir cook till meat to tender and the oil rises to the top, (approximately 30 minutes)

Serves 8   Preparation Time : 30 minutes   Cooking Time : 60 minutes

Pickled Pork

YOU NEED:

○ 2 kgs. lean pork, cleaned ○ 200 gms. salt
○ 1 cup vinegar ○ 15 dried red chillies/peppers
○ 1 teaspoon turmeric powder ○ 1 teaspoon cumin seeds
○ 12 peppercorns ○ 15 cloves garlic ○ ½ cup oil, boiled, cooled.

METHOD:

Dice the cleaned pork into small cubes. Rub half the salt into the meat and keep aside for 12 hours. Then add the remaining salt, turning the meat over. Keep this aside for 2 hours more. In the meantime, grind to a fine paste in the blender/grinder all the spices in vinegar. Wash the meat in a mixture of ½ cup vinegar+2 cups water. Pat dry the washed meat, and spread out on kitchen paper for ½ hour. Now apply the ground spices to the meat, and leave aside for 4 hours. Then heat the oil in a pan on high heat and stir fry the meat continuously in it for 10 minutes. Cool and bottle.

Serves 4   Preparation Time : 35 minutes   Cooking Time : 20 minutes

N.B. *To serve*: Chop fine 1 large onion and 1 large tomato and saute in 1 tablespoon hot oil on medium heat, till light brown. Add 2 tablespoons pickled pork and stir fry for 2 minutes.

Spiced Pork Sausages

YOU NEED:

✪ 4 kgs. pork (boneless) ✪ 2 cups salt
✪ 3 cups vinegar ✪ 1 dessertspoon turmeric powder
✪ 25 dried red chillies/peppers ✪ 2 whole pods garlic
✪ 6 1" pieces ginger ✪ 2 teaspoons peppercorns
✪ 20 cloves ✪ 6 1" pieces cinnamon
✪ 1 tablespoon cumin seeds ✪ 2 metres dried tripe (beef)

METHOD:

Clean the meat, prick it all over with a fork and rub the salt well into the meat. Keep aside for 1 day, putting a weight on it and turning it every 4 hours. After it has been salted for 24 hours, wash the meat well and pat it dry, till no water remains. Grind all the spices, garlic and ginger in vinegar in the blender/grinder. Apply the spices to the meat after cutting it into tiny cubes. Mix well. In the meantime, in flate the dried tripe. Normally, each sausage is about 4" long. Keeping to this, out the tripe into pieces 4½" long. Tie one end of the tripe with a strong piece of string. Fill it with the spiced meat and tie the other end of the sausage likewise. Else fill the spiced meat into the uncut dried tripe, 4" apart, and secure the end of each sausage with the string, so you will have a long string of sausages. Remember to add a little more salt to the spiced meat along with the ground spices, and the remaining vinegar. Dry the sausages in the sun for a week. Store in the refrigerator in a humid climate, or leave open hanging in the pantry/store room.

N.B. To Serve: Put 1 sausage for 2 servings in a pan with enough water to just cover the sausages, along with salt to taste, one tablespoon vinegar, 1 large onion, sliced, 1 large tomato, quartered. Cook it till the oil comes to the top and the water has been absorbed. The prepared sausage is now eaten with pilau, or as a spread between a toasted bun. This is called' chouriz'pau'.

Preparation Time : **2 hours**   *Cooking Time* : **15 minutes**

Pastelão

You Need:

○ 250 gms. pork ○ 250 gms. undercut beef
○ 2 chicken breasts (or 6 chicken legs) ○ 2 spiced pork sausages
○ ½ tablespoon salt ○ 2 tablespoons oil ○ 2 large onions, chopped fine
○ 2 large tomatoes, chopped fine ○ 8 cloves garlic, chopped fine
○ 1" piece ginger, chopped fine ○ 2 cups water
○ ½ cup green peas ○ ½ cup carrots, diced ○ 1 tablespoon vinegar
○ 1 cup boiled, elbow macaroni ○ 2 large potatoes, boiled
○ ½ cup milk ○ ½ teaspoon garam masala
○ salt to taste

Method:

Clean the meat and cut into bite-sized pieces. Apply salt and keep aside for ½ hour. Pressure cook beef and pork for 10 minutes on medium heat in ½ cup water. Heat oil in a pan on medium heat and saute onion, tomatoes, garlic and ginger till a golden brown. Add the pork sausages as well as the pressure cooked meat. Stir-fry for 5 minutes. Now add the chicken pieces, water, potatoes, carrots, macaroni, garam masala and vinegar. Cook on medium flame till water has been reduced to half its quantity. Add the milk and green peas. Cook for 5 minutes till all the ingredients are well combined.

Serves **8**   *Preparation Time* : **20 mins**   *Cooking Time* : **25 mins**

N.B. This dish can be made into a pie. All you have to do is follow the same recipe, but include 4 hard-boiled eggs, quartered, 4 rashers of bacon, fried, the rind removed and the bacon cut into small pieces. Mix both the eggs and the bacon with the cooked dish. Put this pastelao in a baking dish, top with breadcrumbs, a sprinkling of sugar, dotted with butter and covered with a sheet of flaky pastry. Bake at 375°F in a preheated oven till top is golden brown.

Preparation Time : **30 minutes**   *Cooking Time* : **40 minutes**

Girem-mirem

You Need:

✪ 1 kg beef/pork, cut into large cubes ✪ 1 teaspoon salt
✪ 2 tablespoon oil ✪ 1 large onion, chopped fine
✪ 1 large tomato, chopped fine ✪ 4 green chillies, chopped fine
✪ 2 tablespoons coriander leaves, chopped fine
✪ 4 red dried chillies ✪   ½ teaspoon cumin seeds
✪ 10 peppercorns Ground fine in 1 tablespoon vinegar ✪ 1" ginger
✪ ¼ teaspoon turmeric powder

METHOD:

Apply salt to meat and keep aside for 2 hours. Heat oil in a pan on medium flame and saute onion, tomato, green chillies and coriander leaves. Stir fry for 5 minutes. Add the ground spices. Stir-fry for 2 minutes. Now add the meat and stir till the meat is browned. Add 1 cup water and cook on a low flame, till the meat is soft and oil comes to the top which will happen in approximately 30 minutes.

Serves : 6   *Preparation Time* : **20 minutes**   *Cooking Time* : **45 minutes**

Chicken Xacuti (Shakuti)

You Need

○ 1 large chicken (1¼ kgs.) ○ salt to taste
○ 1 cup grated coconut and 1 tablespoon fresh, diced coconut
○ 1½ tablespoon coriander seeds ○ 1 dessertspoon cumin seeds
○ 1 tablespoon poppy seeds ○ 1 teaspoon turmeric powder
○ 8 red dried chillies ○ 8 cloves garlic ○ 1 piece ginger
○ 1 teaspoon grated nutmeg ○ 6 star aniseed ○ 2 teaspoons fennel seeds
○ 1/3 cup oil ○ 2 large onions, chopped fine
○ 6 green-chillies, chopped fine
○ 2 tablespoons tamarind pulp ○ 2 cups water

METHOD:

Wash, clean and joint the chicken, and then cut each piece into two. Apply salt and keep aside. In a flat pan/griddle, on medium heat brown the grated coconut, and all the spices except the nutmeg, green chillies and diced coconut. You will get a strong fragrance when the spices are done (apprx. 3 to 5 mins.) Remove from heat and grind this mixture of roasted spices to a paste in the blender/ grinder. Heat oil in a pan on medium heat and saute all the ground spices along with the green chillies, and 1 large onion chopped fine. Add the chicken pieces, diced, coconut nutmeg and salt to taste along with the tamarind pulp. Lower the flame and add the water gradually, stir cooking, as you do so in an open pan. After 15 minutes, raise the flame and shake the pan gently. The oil will rise to the top. Remove.

Serves **10**   *Preparation Time* **: 25 minutes**   *Cooking Time* **: 30 minutes**

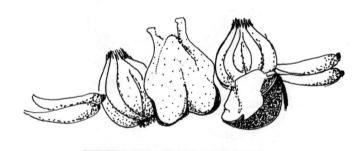

70

(Chicken) Galinha Cafreal

You Need:

✪ 1 large chicken (1¼ kgs.). jointed ✪ 6 green chillies/peppers
✪ 1¼" piece ginger ✪ 10 cloves garlic
✪ 1 tablespoon coriander seeds ✪ 1 teaspoon cumin seeds
✪ ½ teaspoon garam masala ✪ 1 tablespoon lemon juice
✪ 3 tablespoons oil ✪ 2 medium onions, chopped fine
✪ 4 large tomatoes, halved ✪ 6 medium potatoes, boiled, halved

METHOD:
Grind to a fine paste, the ginger, garlic and all the spices in the lemon juice, including the green chillies/peppers and half the chopped onions, adding salt to taste. Joint the chicken and apply the ground spices to the chicken pieces. Marinate the chicken for 2 hours. Heat oil in a pan on medium flame, Saute the rest of the chopped onion. Fry the chicken pieces turning them over so that both sides to the pieces are browned and cooked (approx. 20 mins). In a separate pan, heat 1 tablespoon oil and fry the potatoes and then very lightly the halved tomatoes. Serve the chicken with the fried potatoes and tomatoes.

Serves : 8   *Preparation Time : 30 minutes*   *Cooking Time : 30 minutes*

Chicken Coconut Curry

You Need:

✪ 1 Chicken (1 kg.) jointed ✪ 2 tablespoons oil
✪ 2 medium onions, chopped fine ✪ 2 cups coconut milk
✪ 6 cloves garlic and 1" piece ginger finely ground.
✪ 1 dessertspoon coriander powder ✪ 1 teaspoon cumin powder
✪ 6 green chillies/peppers, slit ✪ 2 large tomatoes, quartered ✪ salt to taste

METHOD:
Heat oil in a deep pan on medium heat. Saute onions to a light golden brown. Mix the powdered and ground spices with the coconut milk green chillies/peppers and tomatoes and cook for 10 minutes. Add salt to taste. Now add the chicken pieces and cook on medium flame, stirring occasionally till a thick consistency is reached. Serve hot with plain, white rice or Coconut Pullao.

Serves : 6   *Preparation Time : 20 minutes*   *Cooking Time : 30 minutes*

Bife de Goa

YOU NEED:

✪ 1 kg beef, undercut ✪ salt to taste ✪ 15 peppercorns, coarsely ground
✪ 8 cloves garlic, chopped fine ✪ 2 large onions ✪ 2 large potatoes ✪ 2 large tomatoes
✪ 2 tablespoons olives oil ✪ 4 red dried chillies/peppers
✪ 2 tablespoons vinegar ✪ 1 cup water

METHOD:

Clean and pat dry the meat. Slice it thinly. Rub in the salt, pepper and garlic in to the meat. Slice the onions, potatoes and tomatoes. Arrange in a deep frying pan, first the sliced onions, then the tomatoes, then the sliced potatoes and lastly the sliced beef. Put the pan on medium heat and pour the olive oil over it also adding the red chillies, chopped roughly. Let it cook for 5 minutes and then pour the vinegar and the water over the meat. Do not stir the meat. Lower the heat cover the pan and let the meat and vegetables simmer till the meat is tender. Shake the pan occasionally. Remove when the sauce is thick and the meat cooked.

Serves 6   Preparation Time : 20 minutes   Cooking Time : 30 minutes

N.B. Chicken or beef can also he used in the recipes given for Pork Vindaloo. 4 cups of soaked (overnight), and boiled Chick peas can be substituted for the chicken xcuti preparation.

Spiced Roast Beef

YOU NEED:

✪ 2 kgs. beef (sirloin) ✪ 8 cloves garlic and 1" piece ginger ground to a fine paste
✪ 1 tablespoon lemon juice ✪ salt to taste ✪ 2 tablespoons oil ✪ 1 cup water
✪ 10 peppercorns ✪ 2" piece cinnamon ✪ 8 cloves ✪ 6 red dried chillies/peppers
✪ 1 tablespoon Worcestershire sauce ✪ 1 dessertspoon cornflour ✪ 4 potatoes, boiled

METHOD:

Clean and pat dry the meat. Prick with a fork and rub in the salt, and garlic-ginger paste and lemon juice. Keep aside under a weight for 6 hours, turning occasionally. Heat oil in a pan on medium heat and brown the meat in the oil. Pressure-cook with 1 cup water peppercorns, cinnamon, cloves, chillies/peppers. When done, remove.

Strain the liquid from the pressure cooker and add the Worcestershire sauce mixed with the cornflour and 2 tablespoons water. Stir cook on low flame till thick. Slice potatoes and meat. Arrange in dish. If preferred the potatoes can be put in the pan along with the meat, peeped and then served pour sauce over the sliced meat. 8 cloves garlic and 1" piece ginger, ground to a fine paste ect.

Serves : 10   Preparation Time : 15 minutes   Cooking Time : 30 minutes

Feijoada

You Need:

○ ½kg. dried black-eyed beans ○ 4 large onions ○ 1 tablespoon vinegar
○ 2 large tomatoes ○ 1 teaspoon recheiado masala ○ 8 clove garlic
○ 1" piece of ginger ○ 1 tablespoon oil ○ 250 gms. pork
○ 4 spiced Goan sausages ○ salt to taste

METHOD:

Soak beans overnight and pressure-cook next morning adding 1 teaspoon oil, 1 tablespoon vinegar and the recheiado masala. Add salt when done (approx. 15 mins.) Cut meat into cubes, add ¼ teaspoon salt and keep aside. Make a paste of the garlic and ginger, cut the onions ad tomatoes fine. Heat the oil on medium flame, and saute the onion. Add the tomatoes and garlic-ginger paste and stir-fry for 10 minutes. Add the meat and the Goan sausages and 1 cup water. Cook on medium flame for 20 minutes, stirring occasionally. Lastly add the cooked beans and cook for another 10 minutes. It' ready now

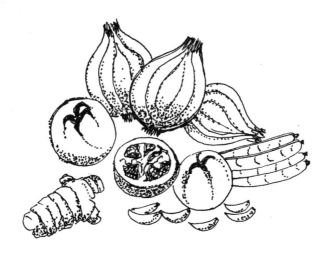

Pickles

Pickles made from green mango are the most popular in Goa. It is made from a variety of recipes, cooked, fresh and sun-cooked. Here are the best ones.

Mango Water-Pickle

You Need:
- 25 small green mangoes (seeds still unformed)
- 2 cups thick kitchen salt ○ 6 red, dried chillies/paprika
- a few peppercorns

METHOD:

Wash and pat dry the mangoes. Arrange the mangoes in a deep pan along with the chillies (whole)/paprika and peppercorns. Sprinkle the salt over all the mangoes and then put a heavy weight over the mangoes. Cover with a muslin cloth. Once a day for 10 days turn the mangoes over. The salt will have melted by now and all the mangoes will be immersed in the salt water. Boil 1 cup water and mix it with ½ cup of the original salt water. Fill a clean, dry, wide-mouthed jar with the salted mangoes and pour the salted liquid over. This pickle is ready after 2 weeks.

Korum

This water pickle is quickly made for daily use.

You Need:
- 1 large green mango ○ 2 green chillies/peppers
- 1 dessertspoon salt ○ 2 tablespoons water

METHOD:

Wash and slice mango, removing the seed. Slit and deseed the green chillies/peppers. Mix all the ingredients and put in a bowl. Keep for 2 hours or more before use.

Preparation Time **: 10 minutes**

Green Mango Chutney

You Need:

- 2 large green mangoes, peeled
- ½ cup grated coconut
- 4 green chillies/peppers, deseeded
- 6 cloves garlic ✿ ½ teaspoon cumin seeds
- 1 tablespoon sugar
- 10 Mint leaves/small sprig of coriander
- juice of 1 lemon ✿ salt to taste

METHOD:

Put all the ingredients in a blender/grinder, after cutting the mangoes into tiny pieces. Blend smooth.

Preparation Time : **10 minutes**

Coconut-Pickled Fish Relish

This relish is particularly appreciated when fish is scarce. It can be eaten with plain rice, a pulao puris or chappatis/unleavened wheat-flour bread baked on a griddle/flat pan.

You Need:

- 1 pickled mackerel ✿ 1 tablespoon oil
- 1 cup grated coconut
- 1 tablespoon tamarind pulp ✿ ½ cup onion, chopped fine
- 2 green chillies/peppers, deseeded, chopped fine
- 2 cloves garlic, chopped fine ✿ 1 teaspoon sugar
- small bunch fresh coriander, chopped fine
- salt to taste

METHOD:

Heat oil in a pan and fry the pickled mackerel on both sides. Debone and shred. Now mix all the ingredients together including the pickled fish.

Preparation Time : **15 minutes**

Coriander Chutney

You Need:

✪ 2 cups coriander leaves, tightly packed
✪ 1 cup fresh, grated coconut ✪ 4 green chillies/peppers
✪ 1 medium onion, chopped fine ✪ ½" piece ginger
✪ 4 cloves garlic ✪ ½ teaspoon cumin seeds
✪ 1 dessertspoon sugar ✪ 1 dessertspoon lemon juice
✪ salt to taste.

METHOD:

Blend all the ingredients in a blender/grinder, adding a tablespoon of water if necessary.

N.B. If coriander is not available, mint leave can be used, or a mixture of both. This chutney goes well on salted biscuits or as a spread for sandwiches. If it is liquefied slightly, it can be used as a dip for French fries, pakoras, or croutons.

Preparation Time : **10 minutes**

Dried Prawn Chutney

You Need:

✪ 1 cup dried prawns ✪ 1 large onion
✪ 4 red dried chillies/peppers ✪ 4 cloves garlic
✪ 1 dessertspoon tamarind pulp ✪ 1 teaspoon sugar
✪ salt to taste

METHOD:

Clean, top and tail the prawns. Roast on a griddle/flat pan to light brown till crisp. Grind the rest of the ingredients together in a blender/grinder. Grind the roasted prawns coarsely and mix with the ground mixture.

Preparation Time : **15 minutes**   *Cooking Time* : **5 minutes**

Chilli/Red Pepper Chutney

You Need:

- 30 red dried chillies/peppers ○ ½ cup lemon juice
- 8 cloves garlic ○ 3 tablespoons sugar
- salt to taste

METHOD:
Grind all the ingredients together in blender/grinder, adding the lemon juice. Vinegar may be used as a substitute for the lemon juice.

Fresh Prawn Balchão

You Need:

- 2 cups of peeled, deveined prawns ○ 2" piece of ginger
- 2 large onion, chopped fine ○ 12 red dried chillies or peppers
- 20 cloves of garlic ○ 1 level dessertspoon turmeric powder
- 1 dessertspoon mustard seeds ○ 1 dessertspoon cumin seeds
- 1 teaspoon peppercorns ○ 20 cloves ○ 2" piece cinnamon
- 1¼ cups vinegar ○ 4 large red tomatoes, chopped fine
- salt to taste ○ 1 cup oil ○ 2 tablespoons sugar

METHOD:
Pat dry the cleaned prawns and marinate them in salt to taste and the turmeric powder, for 1 hour. Grind all the spices, garlic and ginger in vinegar in the blender/grinder. Heat oil in a pan on medium heat. Heat oil in a pan. Stir fry the prawns for 5 minutes. Remove the prawns from the pan, taking care to drain off all the oil. In the same oil, saute the onions and tomatoes till a thick pulp is obtained. To this add the ground spices. Stir fry for, 2 minutes. Add the rest of the ingredients and the prawns. Lower flame and stir cook for a further 5 to 7 minutes till the oil comes to the surface. Cool and bottle. In a humid climate this pickle should be refrigerated.

Preparation Time : **20 minutes**   *Cooking Time* : **15 minutes**

Dried Prawn Balchão

You Need:

✪ 2 cups dried prawns (packed tightly) ✪ 3 large tomatoes
✪ 2 medium onions ✪ ½ cup, oil ✪ 20 large cloves garlic ✪ 2" piece of ginger
✪ 1 tablespoon chilli paprika powder
✪ 1 tablespoon sugar ✪ ½ cup vinegar ✪ ½ cup, oil

Method:

Clean, top and tail the prawns. Heat a griddle or a flat pan and roast the dried prawns, turning continually till they are crisp. Grind coarsely into small pieces. Blanch the tomatoes in hot water, then chop them fine. Chop the onions fine. Heat the oil in a pan on a medium flame. Add the tomatoes and onions and saute till a thick consistency is obtained. Add the garlic and ginger and the chilli or paprika powder. Stir fry for 2 minutes. Add the sugar, vinegar, salt to taste and the dried prawns.Stir cook for a further 5 minutes till all the ingredients have been well combined. Cool and bottle.

Preparation Time : **15 minutes**   *Cooking Time* : **15 minutes**

Mole

For this recipe, usually King Fish or large mackerels are used. A large quantity is normally made to last a year till the next season of plenty comes along in the cold season.

You Need:
- 1½ kgs thickly sliced fish
- 1 heaped dessertspoon turmeric powder
- 1 cup oil ○ 20 red dried chillies or peppers
- 20 cloves garlic ○ 2.2 pieces ginger ○ 1 tablespoon peppercorns
- 10 cloves ○ 2" piece cinnamon
- 1 dessertspoon cumin seeds ○ 1 bottle vinegar (4 cups)
- 1 level tablespoon sugar ○ salt to taste

Method:
Pat dry the fish slices and cut each slice into 4 pieces. Apply salt and turmeric powder over each slice and keep aside for 1 hour. Grind all the spices in a little vinegar in the blender/ grinder, and add the sugar and salt to taste. Heat oil in a pan on medium heat and fry each piece of fish well on both sides. Put the fried fish in a tray in the sun for 2 days, turning the fish pieces twice a day. Now put the ground spices along with the remaining vinegar in a pan on medium heat and boil the contents for 10 minutes. Remove and cool. Arrange the fish in a wide mouthed jar and pour the cooled spiced-vinegar mixture over the fish till the liquid is ½" above the fish pieces. Seal. This pickle is ready to eat after 4 weeks. The longer it is kept, the better it tastes.

Preparation Time : **20 minutes**   *Cooking Time* : **20 minutes**

Pará

You Need:

✪ 24 salted, dried Mackerels
✪ 1½ bottles vinegar ✪ 20 red dried chillies peppers
✪ 10 large cloves garlic ✪ 2,2" pieces ginger
✪ 1 dessertspoon peppercorns ✪ 20 cloves
✪ 2" piece cinnamon
✪ 1 dessertspoon mustard seeds

METHOD:

Remove the heads and the fins of the salted dried mackerels. Wash the fish in 1 cup of vinegar. Grind all the spices except the mustard seeds to a fine paste in vinegar in the blender/or grinder. Heat the rest of the vinegar in a pan on medium heat. When it boils add first the mustard seeds, then the ground spices. Add salt to taste. Cool the spiced vinegar. Now arrange the mackerels in a wide mouthed jar, vertically, till all the fish is tightly packed. Pour the spiced vinegar over the fish, first testing if there is enough salt. Add more if necessary. Seal. This pickle is ready after 4 weeks.

Preparation Time : **25 minutes** *Cooking Time* : **10 minutes**

To serve debone and shred the fish. Heat 1 tablespoon oil (for 1 fish). Lightly fry 1 onion, chopped fine, and 2 green chillies chopped fine. Then add the shredded fish to the onion-chilli mixture, adding salt if necessary. Stir-fry for 1 minute. Remove and serve with a squeeze of lemon.

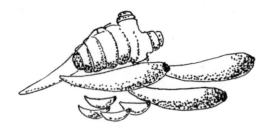

These are the popular cooked pickles made in Goa and used lavishly during the monsoon season when fish is a scarce and an expensive commodity. It is the usual accompaniment to the 'Fish-Curry or Rice' meal.

Mango Pickle

YOU NEED:

- ✪ 50 small green mangoes (their small seed can be removed)
- ✪ 2 cups oil ✪ 1 cup chilli powder, ✪ 1 cup salt
- ✪ 2 tablespoons fenugreek seeds ✪   ½ teaspoon asafoetida

METHOD:
Wash and pat dry the mangoes. Cut the mangoes in quarters only ¾ up from the end till about ¼" from the stem, so each mango is still intact. Stuff each mango with salt and keep for 4 days under a heavy weight. Turn the mangoes once a day. On the 5th. morning, wash the mangoes in the salt brine. Keep aside. Heat ½ cup oil on medium flame in a pan and stir fry all the spices for 2 minutes. Cool and stuff each mango with this spice mixture. Place the mangoes in a wide-mouthed jar, carefully arranged in layers. Cover with the oil which has been previously boiled and cooled.

Preparation Time : **45 minutes**   *Cooking Time* : **2 minutes**

Mango Pickle

YOU NEED:

- ✪ 5 cups diced green mangoes ✪ 1 cup kitchen salt (thick)
- ✪ 20 red dried chillies paprika ✪ 1 level tablespoon turmeric powder
- ✪ 1 heaped tablespoon cumin seeds ✪ 2 tablespoons mustard seeds ✪ 1 teaspoon fenugreek seeds ✪ 2 large pods garlic ✪ 2 2" pieces ginger ✪ 1½ cups sugar
- ✪ 1½ cups vinegar ✪ 1½ cups oil ✪   ¼ teaspoon asafoetida

METHOD:
Peel, pat dry and dice the mangoes into small cubes. Sprinkle them with salt and keep aside for 12 hours. Grind all the spices, garlic and ginger in the vinegar, using more if necessary. Now squeeze out all the liquid from the mango pieces and mix the ground spices and sugar with the mango. Heat the oil in a pan on medium heat with the ¼ teaspoon of asafoetida. Add the mango mixture to the hot oil and stir cook for 10 minutes. Cool, bottle and keep in the sun for 2 weeks.

Preparation Time : **40 minutes**   *Cooking Time* : **12 minutes**

Aubergine (Brinjal) Pickle

YOU NEED:

✪ 1 kg aubergines/brinjals ✪ ½ cup kitchen salt (thick)
✪ 2 2" spices ginger ✪ 4 pods garlic
✪ 1 tablespoon mustard seeds ✪ 2 cups mustard oil
✪ 25 green chillies peppers, chopped into large pieces
✪ 1 level tablespoon turmeric powder ✪ 1 cup sugar
✪ 2 cups vinegar ✪ salt to taste

METHOD:

Wash and pat dry the brinjals and dice them into small cubes. Mix with salt and keep aside for 4 hours. Grind all the spices, garlic and ginger in vinegar in the blender/grinder, Do not add the green chillies peppers. Heat the oil in a pan on a medium flame and stir-fry the ground spices in it. Add the turmeric powder. Now add the remaining vinegar, salt to taste, sugar, chopped green chillies peppers and lastly the brinjals, squeezed dry of all the liquid. Stir-cook for 10 minutes, till the oil comes to the top. Cool and bottle.

Preparation Time : **30 minutes**   *Cooking Time* : **20 minutes**

Lemon Pickle

YOU NEED:

✪ 25 lemons ✪ 20 large cloves garlic
✪ 2,2" pieces ginger ✪ 1½ cups sugar ✪ 2 cups vinegar
✪ 1 level tablespoon chilli powder ✪ salt to taste

METHOD:

Wash and pat dry the lemons. Cut each lemon into 8 pieces, taking care to remove the seeds. Slice the garlic and ginger finally. Put a pan on medium heat, caramelise the sugar to a light brown colour, and add the vinegar gradually to this. Stir cook for 2 minutes. Add the rest of the ingredients to this, and stir cook for a further 10 minutes. Cool and bottle. This pickle is ready after 2 weeks.

Preparation Time : **30 minutes**   *Cooking Time* : **25 minutes**

Tea-Time
Savouries and Sweets

These Tea-Time snacks date back to the leisurely life of the Goan household of yore, when a cup of tea did not suffice at tea-time. It had to be accompanied with one or more savouries or/and sweets. This practice does not hold good today, except if one has the good fortune to have a good cook in the form of a dear grandmother or aunt, staying with one as part of the household, or alternately, an old faithful servant who excels in the culinary art. The wife of today is most often a working person, outside the home as well as inside, and has time during the week for only shop-bought goodies. The weekend may see her turn out some mouth watering delight. But that is a bonus! For those who want to try, here are some favourite recipes.

Empadinhas

For the filling:
You Need:

○ 1 dessertspoon oil ○ 1 medium onion, chopped fine
○ 1 medium tomato, chopped fine ○ 250 gms. pork, diced
○ 250 gms. chicken (breast), diced ○ ½ cup green peas, boiled
○ ¼ cup carrots, diced, boiled ○ ¼ cup potato, diced, boiled
○ 1 stick celery/few mint leaves ○ salt to taste
○ 1 heaped teaspoon cornflour ○ ¼ teaspoon garam masala

Method:

In a pan, on medium heat, put the oil. Saute the onion and tomato till a thick past is obtained. Add the pork and chicken pieces. Stir fry for 2 minutes. Then add rest of the ingredients and stir cook for 10 to 15 minutes. Add the cornflour dissolved in 1 tablespoon water and the garam masala. Stir cook and remove. Cool.

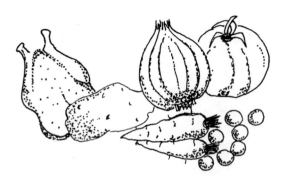

For the Pastry Shells

YOU NEED:

- ○ 2 cups flour, sieved ○ 1 cup semolina
- ○ 1 teaspoon baking powder
- ○ 3 eggs + 1 egg yolk ○ 2 tablespoon sugar
- ○ 2 tablespoons butter

METHOD:

Mix the flour, semolina and baking powder together. Beat the egg yolk together till creamy, adding the sugar gradually and then the butter. Beat the egg whites stiff and add them alternately with the flour-semolina mixture to the egg-butter mixture. Grease 24 deep pastry shells which can hold about 1 tablespoon of filling. Roll out the pastry dough on a floured board. Cut out circles to fit the pastry-shells. Put a dessertspoonful of the mixture into each pastry shell. After putting in the filling, seal the top of each pastry shell with another circle of pastry. Bake at 350° F (180°C), till the pastry tops are a light golden brown. Repeat process till all the filling is used.

Serves : **12** (Makes approximately 30 shells)
Preparation Time : **45 minutes**   *Cooking Time* : **45 minutes**

Merenda

YOU NEED:

- ○ 1 cup whole green lentils (moong)
- ○ 1 cup grated coconut
- ○ ½ cup molasses jaggery
- ○ pinch of salt ○ 1 cup water

METHOD:

Soak the lentils overnight in 2 cups of water. Next morning, drain and wash the lentils. Put all the ingredients together in a pan on a low flame and let the mixture simmer till all the ingredients are well combined, and the Merenda is reduded to half its quantity. Stir cook to prevent it getting burnt at the bottom.

Serves **4**   *Preparation Time* : **10 mintues**   *Cooking Time* : **30 minutes**

Tisana

YOU NEED:

✪ 1 cup nachinim ✪ 1 cup molasses/ jaggery
✪ 1 cup coconut milk ✪ a pinch of salt

METHOD:

Clean and wash the nachinim. Dry it on kitchen paper. Roast the dried nachinim on a griddle or flat pan, then put it in a grinder/mixer and powder it. Now mix it with the rest of the ingredients, put it in a pan on medium heat and stir cook for 15 minutes.

Serves 4   *Preparation Time* : **10 minutes**   *Cooking Time* : **15 minutes.**

Ale Belle

YOU NEED:

✪ 2 eggs ✪ 2 tablespoons butter
✪ 1 cup coconut milk ✪ 1 cup flour ✪   ¼ teaspoon baking powder
✪ salt to taste ✪ butter or oil for cooking

METHOD:

Beat the eggs lightly in a bowl, and gradually add the butter. Beat lightly, adding the coconut milk gradually, then flour with the baking powder, by the spoonful, beating all the time so no lumps are formed. Add salt to taste.

Grease a griddle or a flat pan on medium heat. Mix the butter well and pour a tablespoon of it carefully on the pan, turning the pan around while pouring the butter so the pan is evenly coated. Cook till tiny bubbles appear. Carefully turn over. Remove.

Makes about 12   *Preparation Time* : **15 minutes**   *Cooking Time* : **15 minutes**

For the sauce

YOU NEED:

✪ 1 cup coconut milk ✪ 2 tablespoons molasses/jaggery

Mix the coconut milk and the molasses together and put in a pan on medium heat. Stir cook for 2 minutes. Remove. Arrange the 'Ale Belle' each one folded in four, in a triangle form, in a flat dish. Pour the sauce over it and serve. Or arrange 2 'Ale Belle' in a serving plate for an individual, and pour the sauce over each.

Preparation Time : **10 minutes**   *Cooking Time* : **2 minutes**

Goan Sweets

Goan sweets have their origin in Portugal and the Konkan Region. Portuguese cuisine has had a heady influence on the sweets prepared for festive occasions. A wedding buffet, with its unparalleled display of exotic dishes is often repeated at wedding anniversaries, birthdays and christenings. Tables groaning with food vie with each other for compliments. Recipes from grandmother's days, which have been guarded like family treasures, come out of the vault.

At Christmas, trays of delicacies are produced and consumed. After the Christmas Midnight Mass, held in all the churches, families often visit each other and share a slice of Christmas cake and a glass of wine. The next morning, one sees trays of sweets being exchanged, each tray covered with a home makes a Christmas Crib and a Christmas Star. And each locality has a competition to judge the BEST Star and Crib. To crown it all, there's the Family Christmas Lunch, which has taken long but rewarding hours to prepare with each (member) of the family having a lick of as it is being prepared, and each one giving their opinion. Festive table is deemed complete without the famous sorpotel and bibinca.

Every Goan sweet has coconut in its thinly sliced or milked form Goan sweets take time and talent to prepare, but the end results are most gratifying, and are sure to draw many a compliment. Experience, however, is what ensures results. Keep at it. The compliments will come.

Bibinça

You Need:

○ 1 kg castor sugar
○ 3 cups coconut milk (extract of 2 coconuts)
○ 20 egg yolks ○ 100 gms. flour
○ ½ teaspoon grated nutmeg
○ 2 teaspoons cardamom essence
○ 1 cup clarified butter (ghee)

Method:

Mix the castor sugar with the coconut milk till dissolved. Beat egg yolks till creamy, and add to the coconut milk and mix the flour in it thoroughly, without any lumps. Add this to the mixture of coconut milk, sugar and eggs, along with the nutmeg and cardamom. Take a deep pan, about 6" in diameter and put a tablespoon of clarified butter in it. Put it under a grill (medium heat). Take it out of the grill and pour enough batter into the pan to cover the bottom about ¼" in thickness. Put under the grill for about 2 minutes and let it cook till it is a deep brown in colour. Remove from grill, put a dessertspoonful or clarified butter over the cooked layer, following it with enough batter to cover the first layer, about ¼" thick. Repeat this process till all the batter and clarified butter has been used up in the same way. The batter must always be in the same proportion. The last layer has to be the clarified butter. When cool, turn out onto a dish, keeping the first layer face down. Decorate the last layer with a few slivers of toasted almonds if desired. To serve, cut into thin slices.

Serves **25**   *Preparation Time* : **30 minutes**   *Cooking Time* : **30 minutes.**

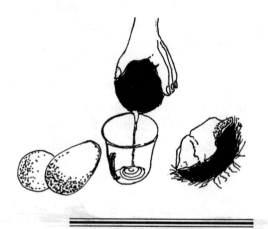

Potato Bibinça

This is the poorer version of the famous bibinca, but nontheless delectable.

You Need:

- ½ kg boiled potatoes
- 2 cups coconut milk (extract of 1½ coconuts)
- 2½ cups castor sugar ✪ 100 gms. flour ✪ 4 large eggs
- ¼ teaspoon grated nutmeg ✪ 1 teaspoon cardamom essence
- ½ cup clarified butter (ghee) ✪ sliced glace cherries

METHOD:

Sieve the boiled potatoes. Dissolve the sugar in the coconut milk by stirring gently. Add the flour to the coconut milk, making sure there are no lumps. Beat the egg whites stiff and add to the beaten egg yolks. Now mix all the ingredients together making a thick batter. Follow the instructions cooking this potato Bibinca, as the earlier Bibinca. Decorate with sliced glace cherries.

Preparation Time : **20 minutes**   *Cooking Time* : **30 minutes**

Sans Rival (a delicious cake)

You Need:

- 9 eggs whites ✪ 350 gms. castor sugar
- 450 gms. almonds, ground fine
- 1 teaspoon baking powder. ✪ 1 cup cream,
- a few almonds and cherries.

METHOD:

Beat the egg whites stiff, till they stand up in peaks. Now, very gradually, add the sugar, beating continuously. Lastly beat in the ground almonds and the baking powder...Set the oven at 350°F. (180°C) and when it is hot, grease 2 small flat baking trays and divide the mixture in half, putting half in each tray. Bake till the tops are a faint golden in colour. Remove and cool. Beat the cream manually in a blender till it is fairly thick. Sandwich the 2 baked portions together, and decorate with the almonds and cherries. To serve, cut in slices.

Serves : **8**   *Preparation Time* : **10 minutes**   *Cooking Time* : **15 minutes**

A Letria

You Need:

✪ ½ kg sugar ✪ 2 cups water ✪ 6 egg yolks
✪ 3 cups grated coconut
✪ 4 slices fresh bread, cut into tiny cubes, minus the crusts
✪ 2 teaspoons Almond essence ✪ 2 tablespoons raisins
✪ a few almonds for decoration

METHOD:

In a large, rounded karhai or pan on medium heat stir the sugar and water together till the sugar is completely dissolved. Lower the flame while you beat the egg yolks till they are creamy. Put the egg yolk mixture into an icing bag with a thin nozzle. Increase the heat to medium and drizzle the egg yolk mixture over the sugar syrup in a cobweb pattern, till all the egg yolk mixture has been used. Remove the pan and very carefully with 2 forks lift off the egg yolk cobweb and keep aside carefully. Now put the pan back on medium heat and add the coconut, bread and essence to the sugar syrup. Stir cook continuously till all the sugar syrup has been absorbed, about 15 minutes. Remove the pan and put the mixture onto a flat serving dish. When cool, in a mound on the dish, with the raisins and almonds over the top and sides.

Serves : 10 *Preparation Time* : **15 minutes** *Cooking Time* : **25 minutes**

Cocada (Coconut sweet)

You Need:

✪ 4 cups grated coconut ✪ 1 cup water
✪ 2½ cups sugar ✪ 2 cups semolina
✪ 2 teaspoons almond cardamom essence

METHOD:

Grind the grated coconut finely in a blender/grinder. Keep aside. Pure the water and sugar together in a pan on medium heat and stir cook till the sugar has dissolved. Take off the heat and add the rest of the ingredients to the pan. Put the pan on medium heat again and stir cook till a thick consistency is obtained, (approximately 15 minutes). Remove pan and turn out contents onto a flat greased surface. Cool and cut into diamond shapes. If this sweet is to be eaten later, then store in an airtight tin in the refrigerator.

Serves : 12 *Preparation Time* : **15 minutes** *Cooking Time* : **25 minutes**

Doce de Grão (A Soft Halwa)

You Need:

○ ½ kg split chick peas (channa dal)
○ 2 cups grated coconut ○ ½ kg. sugar ○ 2 cups water
○ 2 tablespoon butter ○ 1 teaspoon cardamom essence

Method:
Wash the chick peas and soak them overnight. Drain the next morning. Grind the coconut in a blender/grinder. Keep aside. In the water and put in a pan on medium heat. Stir cook till the sugar has been dissolved and a thick syrup has been obtained. Remove from heat and carefully mix in the ground coconut, ground chick peas, butter and essence. Stir cook continuously (so the bottom does not burn), till the Doce de Grao is thick and leave the sides of the pan. Turn out onto a greased, flat surface and flatten out the mixture to about ½" in thickness. When it cools, cut into diamond shapes and store in an airtight jar in the refrigerator after the first day.

Serves : 12   *Preparation Time* : **15 minutes**   *Cooking Time* : **40 minutes**

Doce de Grão (2)

You Need:

○ 750 gms. split chick peas (channa dal)
○ 3 cups grated coconut ○ 2 cups water
○ 200 gms. butter ○ 1 kg. castor sugar
○ 8 eggs. separated ○ 750 gms. semolina
○ 1 cup cashewnuts, roasted & sliced
1 teaspoon vanilla essence.

Method:
Wash and soak chick peas overnight. Next morning, boil them in the same water and grind to a fine consistency. Keep aside. Grind the coconut fine and mix it with the chick peas mixture. Cream together the butter and sugar, add and the beaten egg yolks to it. Mix in the semolina. Now beat the egg whites stiffly and add to the above mixture. Keep aside for 4 hours. Add the essence and nuts now and put into a greased flat baking dish. Bake at 375°F/180°C for 45 minutes or till golden brown in colour and well risen. Cool and serve in slices.

Serves : 8   *Preparation Time* : **30 minutes**   *Cooking Time* : **45 minutes**

Bolinhas (Cookies)

You Need:
✪ 8 egg yolks ✪ 2 cups castor sugar
✪ 3 cups semolina
✪ 3 cups cashewnuts, ground
✪ 1 teaspoon cardamom or almond essence
✪ 4 cups grated coconut, ground fine

Method:
Beat the egg yolks till thick and creamy. Mix the egg yolks with the sugar, semolina, ground cashewnuts and essence. Keep aside for 8 hours. Now add the coconut and mix thoroughly. Shape into small balls (approximately 24), flattened slightly at the bottom. Bake in an oven heated to 375°F./180°C, till the Bolinhas are light golden brown.

Serves : 10   Preparation Time : 25 minutes   Cooking Time : 25 minutes

Bolo de Rulão (a cake)

You Need:
✪ ¾ cup butter ✪ 2 ½ cups castor sugar
✪ 6 large eggs ✪ 3½ cups coconut, grated and ground fine
✪ ½ kg. semolina ✪ 1 heaped teaspoon baking powder
✪ ¼ teaspoon salt ✪ 2 teaspoons rose essence

Method:
Cream butter and sugar till light and fluffy. Separate egg yolks and beat them till creamy. Add this to the butter-sugar mixture. Beat egg whites stiff and add to the creamed mixture alternately with the ground coconut, semolina baking powder, salt and essence. If needed, you may add a tablespoon of milk. Leave overnight in a cool place. Bake in an oven preheated to 375°F., 180°C till well risen and light golden brown in colour.

N.B. Instead of Rose essence, you may substitute almond essence.

Serves : 10   Preparation Time : 25 minutes   Cooking Time : 40 minutes

Bolo (a cake)

You Need:

- ¾ cup sugar   ¾ cup water
- ½ cup semolina   3 eggs, separated
- 2 cups grated coconut, ground fine
- 1 teaspoon baking powder
- 1 teaspoon almond essence.

METHOD:
Make a syrup of the sugar and water (one thread consistency). Cool and then add the semolina. Keep aside for 3 hours. Beat the egg yolks till creamy. Then beat the egg whites stiff. Add the beaten eggs to the semolina mixture. Finally add the coconut, baking powder and essence. This is the filling for the pastry.

Pastry

You Need:

- ¾ cup flour
- 1 tablespoon butter
- Enough water to make a stiff dough.

METHOD:
Mix all the ingredients together to form a stiff dough. Roll out thinly on a floured board. Line a 1 kg baking pan with this pastry, keeping a little for decorating the top. Roll out the remaining dough and cut into strips. After filling in the semolina mixture into the pastry lined baking pan, level the top and decorate it with the strips in a criss-cross design. Bake in a preheated oven 375°F./180°c till the top is a golden-brown colour.

Serves : 10   *Preparation Time* : 20 minutes   *Cooking Time* : 40 minutes

Rose de Coque (Cookies)

YOU NEED:

✪ 3 eggs ✪ 4 tablespoons flour
✪ 1 cup milk ✪ 2 tablespoons castor sugar ✪ vanilla essence ✪ 3 cups oil
✪ flower form for making the Rose do Coques

METHOD:

Beat the eggs till, creamy then add the flour, milk and sugar gradually, mixing it gently all the time. No lumps should be formed. The consistency should be of a thickish, pouring one. Heat oil in a deep pan on medium heat. Now dip the Rose de Coque form into the hot oil, completely submerging it, for 1 minute. Now remove the form and immediately dip into the batter uptil 2 tenths of an inch below the top of the form. This to allow the Rose de Coque to slip off the form easily, with a tap on the form, when it is ready. Now remove the form from the hot oil, tap the form with a spoon and allow the fried Rose de Coque to slip onto a sheet of kitchen paper so that the oil will be absorbed. The Rose de Coque should be crisp. Do likewise for the rest of the batter. Cool and store in an airtight jar.

Serves : **12**   *Preparation Time* : **15 minutes**   *Cooking Time* : **40 minutes**

N.B. This form can be used in a store selling kitchen equipment.

Pasteis de Stª Clara
(Tarts)

YOU NEED:

✪ 250gms. butter ✪ 200gms. castor sugar
✪ 350gms. flour ✪ a pinch salt ✪ 1 teaspoon vanilla essence ✪ 1 egg
✪ 1 cup Mixed Fruit Jam

METHOD:

Cream butter and sugar together till light and creamy. Beat the egg well and add to the butter-sugar mixture. Now add the salt and essence and gradually the flour till a soft, stiff dough is obtained. Roll out dough on a floured board, 1 cm. in thickness. Cut into circles to fit into a tart tray. Grease the tart tray and then press a round of pastry into each tart form. Fill each with a teaspoonful of jam and do a single criss-cross over each tart. Bake in an oven preheated to 375°F/180°C for 15 minutes. Remove, cool and store in an airtight container. Makes 24 tarts.

Preparation Time : **30 minutes**   *Cooking Time* : **15 minutes**

Nankatais

YOU NEED:

○ 1 kg. flour ○ a pinch of salt
○ ¼ kg. castor sugar ○ ½ kg. clarified butter (ghee)
○ vanilla/almond essence

METHOD:

Sieve the salt and flour together and, add the sugar. Mix well. Rub in the essence with the clarified butter, with heel of your palm, till the mixture is smooth and soft to the touch (approximately 40 minutes). Form the dough into small balls, flattening the bottom slightly by pressing the balls lightly onto the baking tray. Press a sliver of almond or cashewnut or half crystallised cherry into the centre of each Nankatai. Bake in an oven preheated to 375°F, on a greased baking tray with the Nankatais ½" apart, for 25 minutes, till a very light golden brown in colour. Cool and store in an airtight jar. Makes about 36 Nankatais.

Preparation Time : **45 minutes** *Cooking Time* : **25 minutes**

Coconut Macaroons

YOU NEED:

○ 3 egg whites ○ 2 tablespoons castor sugar
○ 2 tablespoons flour (heaped) ○ 1 cup coconut, grated
○ ½ teaspoon baking powder
○ 1 teaspoon vanilla/almond essence

METHOD:

Whip egg whites stiffly. Beat the sugar into them, then add the flour gradually followed by the rest of the ingredients, beating each in turn into the mixture till it stands up in peaks. In a preheated oven, 300°F, put spoonfuls of the mixture on a greased baking tray, 1" apart, and bake till the coconut macaroons are a light golden brown in colour, about 20 minutes.

This quantity makes about 24 macaroons.

Preparation Time : **15 minutes** *Cooking Time* : **20 minutes**

Dodol (a soft halwa)

You Need:

✪ 250 gms raw rice ✪ 4 cups coconut, grated
✪ 375 gms. Coconut molasses (jaggery)
✪ ½ cup cashewnuts, chopped coarsely
✪ 1 tablespoon butter ✪ 1 teaspoon Vanilla essence

Method:

Wash and soak rice overnight. Next morning grind fine in a blender/grinder and keep aside. Extract 3 cups thick coconut milk from the grated coconut. Mix the coconut milk with the rest of the ingredients until well combined. In a deep pan, on medium heat, stir cook the Dodol continuously, till it is reduced to half its quantity and starts leaving the sides of the pan. This will take about 45 minutes or less. Turn out contents onto a flat dish/plate. Cool. Serve in thick slices.

Serves : 8   *Preparation Time* : **25 minutes**   *Cooking Time* : **45 minutes**

Doce Baji (A soft halwa)

You Need:

✪ 2 cups broken wheat grains
✪ 3 cups coconut, grated ✪ ½ cup sugar ✪ 1 tablespoon butter
✪ 1 teaspoon vanilla essence
✪ ½ cup cashewnuts, chopped coarsely

Method:

Wash and soak wheat in 2 cups water, overnight. Next morning, add another cup of water to the wheat and pressure cook it. The wheat will now be soft. Remove from the heat. Extract 2 cups thick coconut milk from the grated coconut. Mix the wheat, sugar and coconut milk together. Put in a deep pan on medium heat and stir cook till the mixture is reduced to half its quantity. Now add the rest of the ingredients and stir cook continuously till the mixture leaves the sides of the pan, about 15 minutes. Turn out onto a greased, flat serving dish. Cool. Dhos Bhaji is eaten in small serving plates, cut in thick wedges.

Serves : 12   *Preparation Time* : **20 minutes**   *Cooking Time* : **45 minutes**

Dedos de Damas

You Need

✿ ½ kg. sugar ✿ 1 cup water ✿ ½ kg. almonds, roasted & ground fine
✿ 1 egg white ✿ 1 cup sugar ✿ 1 dessertspoon water

METHOD:

Put the ½ kg. sugar and 1 cup water in a pan on medium heat and stir cook till a thick consistency is obtained (one thread). Stir in ground almonds and stir cook for 15 minutes till well combined. Remove from heat. Cool and mix in unbeaten egg white. Return to pan and on low heat stir cook till the mixture is thick and leaves the sides of the pan. Turn out on to a greased flat surface and knead with the heel of the palm of your hand, gently, till the mixture is dry and smooth. Shape into small cocktail sausages. Keep aside for 12 hours. Caramelise 1 cup sugar and 1 dessertspoon water. Dip each Dedos de Damas in to the caramelised sugar while the sugar is still warm. Put a long toothpick into the centre of each Dedos de Damas from one end and decorate the toothpick with a white paper frill twisted around the toothpick. Arrange the Dedos de Damas artistically on a big grapefruit/small, watermelon. You should get about 30 Dedos de Damas.

N.B. If long toothpicks are difficult to obtain, take a piece of bamboo, 6" long, and fashion the toothpicks from it.

Preparation Time : **15 minutes**   *Cooking Time* : **25 minutes**

Teias de Aranhas
(Cobweb Coconut Cookies)

You Need
○ 4 young coconuts ○ 2 cups sugar
○ ½ cup water ○ A few drops red food colouring ○ 1 teaspoon vanilla essence

METHOD:

With a sharp knife cut the coconut flesh in thin strips, trying to cut each strip as long as the radius of the coconut. Make a syrup of the sugar and water (one thread consistency), in a pan on medium heat, adding the essence and a few drops of red food colour, to make the syrup a light pink colour. Remove pan from heat, and dip each strip of coconut into the syrup. On a small circle of butter paper, arrange two strips of Teias de Aranhas in a circular cobweb pattern. Leave the completed Teias de Aranhas in a dry place to harden. This will take at least 6 hours. Store carefully in an airtight tin. These Teias de Aranhas should be consumed quickly. You may use different food colours to make them more interesting. Makes about 24 Teias de Aranhas.

Preparation Time : **25 minutes** *Cooking Time* : **25 minutes**

Feos de Ovos

You Need:
○ 10 eggs, separated ○ A few drops yellow food colouring
○ 1½ cups sugar ○ 1/3 cup water ○ 2½ tablespoons castor sugar
○ 2½ tablespoons cornflour ○ a few almonds and cherries for decoration

METHOD:

Add the yellow food colouring to the egg yolks and beat them till creamy. Strain the egg yolks through a strainer. Keep aside. Put the sugar and water in a pan on medium heat and bring it to a boil. Stir cook this sugar mixture till it is slightly thickened, (approximately 5 minutes) Put the strained egg yolk mixture into an icing bag with a thin nozzle. Now drizzle the egg yolk mixture over the sugar syrup in circles covering the whole area. Remove the egg yolk strands carefully when the syrup has cooled. Keep aside. Whisk egg whites stiffly and fold in the castor egg whites. Pour this mixture into a greased, round baking tin, and place this tin in a larger pan with 1 cup water in it on high flame for 5 minutes, then lower the flame to medium for another 5 minutes, till the Feos de Ovos is well set. Cool and invert on to a serving dish. Cover the top with the egg yolk strands and decorate with almonds and cherries.

Serves : **10** *Preparation Time* : **10 minutes** *Cooking Time* : **15 minutes**

Doce de Castanhas (Goan Barfi)

YOU NEED:

○ 3¾ cups sugar ○ 1 cup water
○ 4 cups roasted cashewnuts, ground fine
○ a few drops green food colouring
○ 1 teaspoon rose essence

METHOD:

Put the sugar and water together in a deep pan on medium flame. When a thick syrup has been obtained by stir cooking for 10 minutes or so, gradually add the rest of the ingredients. Stir cook continuously till a thick consistency has been obtained (approximately 15 minutes) Pour the contents onto a flat greased surface and when cool, cut into diamond shapes.

Serves : 10   *Preparation Time* : 10 minutes   *Cooking Time* : 25 minutes

Neurios

YOU NEED:

○ ½ kg. flour ○ salt to taste
○ 4 tablespoons water ○ 3 cups oil for frying

For the filling:

○ ½ cup small raisins ○ ½ cup cashewnuts, chopped fine
○ 1 cup grated coconut, roasted lightly on a griddle
○ 1 tablespoon sesame seeds, lightly roasted
○ ½ cup granulated sugar ○ ¼ teaspoon cardamom powder

METHOD:

Mix sieved flour and salt with the water to make a soft dough. Roll out the dough thinly on a floured board. Take a 2" biscuit cutter and cut out circles from the rolled out dough. Now, in a bowl, gently mix together all the ingredients for the filling. Put a teaspoonful of this filling onto one-half of the circle. Moisten the edge of the circle and gently press it over the filling to form a semi-circle. Press the tines of a fork round the edge of the neurio. Do likewise for the rest of the rounds till all the dough has been used. Heat the oil on a medium flame, and when it is very hot, lower the flame. Deep fry the neurios in the hot oil, turning them over till both sides are a golden brown. Cool and store in an airtight jar.

Serves : 10   *Preparation Time* : 45 minutes   *Cooking Time* : 40 minutes.

Kulkuls

You Need:
- ½ kg flour, sieved ○ pinch of salt
- 1 tablespoon butter, cold ○ 2 egg yolks
- 3 tablespoons castor sugar ○ 1 cup thick coconut milk ○ 3 cups oil, for frying

METHOD:

Mix flour and salt and, add the butter, cut into pieces. Mix gently, then add the egg yolks, which have been beaten. Add the sugar and coconut milk now and mix the dough till it is pliable and soft. Form small marble sized balls of the dough. Grease the cines of a fork and flatten out the marble-sized dough with it, then roll up the flattened dough from one side to them. It should resemble a tight curl. Heat the oil in a deep pan on medium flame, and fry the kulkuls in it, turning them over till they are light golden brown in colour. Carefully remove the fried kulkuls from the hot oil.

N.B. You may like to cover the kulkuls in sugar. To do this, you have to cook 1 cup sugar with 4 tablespoons water in a pan on medium heat. Stir cook the syrup for 5 minutes till it thickness. Now toss the kulkuls carefully in this syrup, after you have taken it off the heat. Cool and store in an airtight jar.

Serves : 12   Preparation Time : 50 minutes   Cooking Time : 40 minutes

Doce de Coco

You Need
- 2 slices fresh bread ○ 500 gms. sugar
- ½ cup water ○ 4 cups finely grated coconut
- 1 tablespoon butter ○ a few drops red food colouring ○ almond essence
- ½ cup almonds/cashewnuts, roasted & chopped coarsely

METHOD:

Cut the bread into tiny cubes, minus the crusts. Pu the water and sugar together in a deep pan on medium heat and stir cook till the sugar is dissolved. Add the bread cubes and cubes and coconut. Stir cook continuously for 10 minutes, till the mixture is thick. Now add the butter, food colouring (enough to make it a light pink), essence and nuts. Stir cook for a further 5 minutes; the mixture will start leaving the sides of the pan. Turn out onto a greased flat surface. Cool and cut into small diamond shapes.

Serves : 8   Preparation Time : 15 minutes   Cooking Time : 20 minutes

N.B. This can be made in 2 colours, one layer over the other.

Perada (Guava Cheese)

YOU NEED:
- ✪ 1 kg. large, seedless guavas
- ✪ 6 cups water ✪ 750 gms. sugar
- ✪ juice of 2 lemons
- ✪ 2 tablespoons butter ✪ pinch of salt

METHOD:
Wash and cut guavas into small pieces. Put into a deep pan along with the water on medium heat. Stir cook till the pieces have been reduced to half the quantity and are pulpy. Remove from heat and sieve the pulp through a fine sieve, so the seeds and skin are removed. Now put the pulp back into the pan with the rest of the ingredients and stir cook continuously till the pulp is thick and begins to leave the sides of the pan. This is a laborious process but very rewarding! Take off heat and put the mixture onto a flat surface. Flatten the perada to about ½" in thickness. When cool, cut into diamond shapes. Store in a container with butter paper between each layer.

Serves : 10   *Preparation Time* : 40 minutes   *Cooking Time* : 45 minutes

Pinaca

YOU NEED:
- ✪ 1 kg. boiled rice
- ✪ ¼ kg. green lentils (moong) ✪ 500 gms. coconut molasses (jaggery)
- ✪ 2 tablespoons water ✪ 4 coconuts, grated

METHOD:
Roast the rice and green lentils on a griddle on medium flame. Put in a blender/grinder and grind to a fine paste. Keep aside. Combine the water and molasses and put in a pan on medium heat and stir cook till the molasses have dissolved. Add the grated coconut to the above mixture and cook in the pan on medium heat till all the liquid has been absorbed, and the mixture is quite dry. Put this mixture in to a blender/grinder and reduce to a thick paste. Now mix this with the powdered rice and green lentil powder till all the ingredients have been well combined. Form the Pinaca into cocktail sausage size pieces and keep on an open tray to dry out for a few hours. Store in a an airtight tin. It can also be pressed into small cookie forms. The finished product should weigh about 2¾ kgs.

Serves : 12   *Preparation Time* : 20 minutes   *Cooking Time* : 30 minutes

Mangada

YOU NEED:

- ✪ 4 cups mango pulp (about 10 large mangoes)
- ✪ 3½ cups sugar ✪ 1 tablespoon butter
- ✪ 1 teaspoon cardamom essence

METHOD:

Take just ripe mangoes and extract the pulp equal to 4 cups. The mangoes must be of the good eating quality. In Goa, the Mangada is usually made from the 'Musaraat' variety. But any good quality mango can be used. Put the mango pulp, sugar butter and cardamom together in a deep pan on medium flame. Stir cook till the mixture boils for 30 minutes, and the Mangada is reduced to less than half the quantity, and starts leaving the sides of the pan. Stir cook continuously. Turn out the contents onto a flat greased surface. When cool, cut into cubes and store in an airtight container.

N.B. If you want the Mangada to be eaten as a jam, which is delicious, then reduce the quantity of sugar to 2 cups. Remove the jam when it is half the original quantity. Bottle when cool.

Serves : 12   Preparation Time : 20 minutes   Cooking Time : 45 minutes

Figado (Banana Halwa)

YOU NEED:

- ✪ 3 cups banana pulp, yellow variety ✪ 2½ cups sugar
- ✪ 2 tablespoons clarified butter (ghee)
- ✪ ¼ teaspoon cinnamon powder
- ✪ pinch of citric acid

METHOD:

Mix all the ingredients together till they are well combined. Put into a deep pan on medium beat and stir continuously till the mixture thickens and leaves the sides of the pan. Turn out onto a flat greased surface. Cool and cut into diamond shapes. Store in an airtight container. You may add a few drops of green food colouring to make the Figado more interesting.

Serves : 8   Preparation Time : 5 minutes   Cooking Time : 20 minutes

Doce de Pao

You Need:

- 8 large slices of fresh bread
- 1 cup milk ✪ 3 egg yolks
- grated lemon rind of 1 lemon ✪ 4 tablespoons sugar
- ¼ teaspoon powdered cinnamon
- 1 tablespoon butter

METHOD:

Remove the crusts from the bread slices. Cut the bread into tiny cubes. Heat the milk, remove from heat and soak the bread in the hot milk. Put the milk soaked bread in the pan on medium heat and stir cook till the bread is pulpy. Beat the egg yolks and put them with the rest of the ingredients into the pan. Stir cook continuously, till the Doce de Pao leaves the sides of the pan. Turn out onto a flat serving dish and arrange with the cinnamon sprinkled over it. Served it in wedges.

Serves **: 6**   *Preparation Time* **: 10 minutes**   *Cooking Time* **: 15 minutes**

Bol Raina

You Need:

- ✪ 300 gms. clarified butter (ghee)
- ✪ 2 cups castor sugar ✪ 4 eggs, separated
- ✪ 2 cups flour, sieved ✪ 1 cup milk
- ✪ ½ teaspoon baking powder
- ✪ 1 teaspoon vanilla essence

METHOD:

In a bowl mix the clarified butter and sugar together. Beat the egg yolks till creamy and add to the clarified butter-sugar mixture. Beat egg whites stiff and add it to the mixture alternately with the flour till all the egg whites and flour have been used. Fold in the milk, baking powder and essence. Put in a greased baking tin, and bake in an oven preheated 375°F/190° till the Bol Raina is well risen and golden brown on top. This should take about 30 minutes.

Serves : 8   *Preparation Time* : **10 minutes**   *Cooking Time* : **30 minutes**